W9-ACZ-083

ELMORE LEONARD

LITERATURE AND LIFE: MYSTERY WRITERS
A selected list of titles:

Arthur Conan Doyle by Don Richard Cox

Raymond Chandler by Jerry Speir

P. D. James by Norma Siebenheller

The Murder Mystique: Crime Writers on Their Art edited by Lucy Freeman

Sons of Sam Spade: The Private Eye Novel in the 70s by David Geherin

Rex Stout by David R. Anderson

Dashiell Hammett by Dennis Dooley

Michael Innes by George L. Scheper

The American Private Eye: The Image in Fiction by David Geherin

John le Carré by Peter Lewis

13 Mistresses of Murder by Elaine Budd

The Secret of the Stratemeyer Syndicate: Nancy Drew, The Hardy Boys, and the Million Dollar Fiction Factory by Carol Billman

Dick Francis by Melvyn Barnes

James M. Cain by Paul Skenazy

Eric Ambler by Peter Lewis

The Literature of Crime and Detection by Waltraud Woeller and Bruce Cassiday

Complete list of titles available from the publisher on request.

ELMORE LEONARD

David Geherin

A Frederick Ungar Book
CONTINUUM · NEW YORK

1989

The Continuum Publishing Company
370 Lexington Avenue
New York, NY 10017

Printed in the United States of America

Library of Congress Cataloging-in-Publication Data

Geherin, David, 1943–
Elmore Leonard / by David Geherin.
p. cm.—(Literature and life. Mystery writers)
"A Frederick Ungar book."
Bibliography: p.
Includes index.
ISBN 0-8264-0420-0
1. Leonard, Elmore, 1925– . 2. Novelists, American—20th century—Biography. 3. Detective and mystery stories, American—History and criticism. 4. Crime and criminals in literature.
I. Title. II. Series.
PS3562.E55Z68 1989
813′.54—dc19
[B] 88-26697
CIP

For My Parents
and To the Memory of Blanche Taylor

Contents

Preface

There are two types of success stories in America: the flashy overnight sensation, who all too often fades just as quickly as he rises to fame; and the long-overdue success, who usually enjoys a more lasting reputation. Elmore Leonard definitely belongs to the second group. Critical and popular recognition were slow in coming to Leonard. "Novelist Discovered after Twenty-Three Books" is how a *New York Times* headline put it in a 1983 profile of his work. But this lack of attention had its positive side: it gave Leonard the opportunity to develop his craft away from the spotlight. When critics and readers finally caught up with him in the early 1980s, they discovered that he had quietly, without fanfare, produced a body of work that raised the crime novel to new levels of artistry. His subsequent novels have only solidified his reputation as one of America's greatest crime writers.

The following book opens with a biography of Leonard. Chapter 2 is devoted to the western novels and short stories he published in the 1950s. Chapter 3 deals with his transition from westerns to crime novels in the 1960s. Chapters 4 through 6 provide in-depth treatments of the fifteen major crime novels he wrote between *Fifty-Two Pickup* in 1974 and *Freaky Deaky* in 1988. Chapter 7 is devoted to a consideration of his artistry.

I would like to express my appreciation to the following individuals for their invaluable assistance in this project: first of all, to Elmore Leonard, for being so generous with his time in talking with me about his work; to Gregg Sutter and Bill Marshall, for sharing information about their behind-the-scenes roles in assisting Leonard in his research; to Joel Lyczak, who lent me copies of several of Leonard's hard-to-find pulp stories; to Ms. Kroll of the University of Detroit Library, who guided me through the material in the Elmore Leonard collection there; and to my editor, Bruce Cassiday, for his support of the book.

Chronology

1925 October 11, Elmore Leonard born in New Orleans, Louisiana.

1934 After several moves, his family settles in Detroit.

1943 Graduates from high school. Drafted into the navy and serves with the Seabees in New Guinea and Admiralty Islands.

1946 Returns home. Enrolls at University of Detroit, where he majors in English and philosophy.

1949 Marries Beverly Cline.

1950 Graduates from University of Detroit. Begins working as an office boy at Campbell-Ewald Advertising in Detroit. Later becomes a copywriter.

1951 First story, "Trail of the Apache," published in *Argosy*. Begins routine of writing between 5 A.M. and 7 A.M. each morning before leaving for work.

1953 First novel, *The Bounty Hunters,* is published.

1954 *The Law at Randado.*

1956 *Escape from Five Shadows*

1957 Two films, *3:10 to Yuma* and *The Tall T,* based on Leonard's western pulp stories, are released.

1959 *Last Stand at Saber River.*

1961 *Hombre.* Quits job at Campbell-Ewald with hopes of becoming a full-time writer. Ends up doing free-lance work writing educational and industrial films.

1965 Twentieth Century-Fox purchases film rights to *Hombre* for 10,000 dollars, which finally allows Leonard to give up free-lance work and devote himself to writing fiction.

1966 H. N. Swanson becomes Leonard's agent.

1969 *The Big Bounce,* Leonard's first non-western novel, is published. He also sells his first screenplay, based on his Prohibition-era novel, *Mr. Majestyk.*

1970 *Valdez is Coming.*

1972 Leonard's first original screenplay, *Joe Kidd,* starring Clint Eastwood, is released.

1974 *Mr. Majestyk,* a Charles Bronson film based on Leonard's original screenplay, is released. In addition to his novelization of the screenplay, *Fifty-Two Pickup* is also published. Separates from his wife.

1976 *Swag.*

1977 *Unknown Man No. 89.* Quits drinking. Divorced from his wife.

1978 *The Switch.* Does extensive research into the Detroit Police for a profile he writes for the *Detroit News.*

1979 *Gunsights,* his final western novel, is published. Marries Joan Shepard.

1980 *Gold Coast,* first Florida novel, and *City Primeval,* first novel to feature a police hero, are published.

1981 *Split Images*. Gregg Sutter begins working as Leonard's researcher.

1982 *Cat Chaser*.

1983 *Stick* and *LaBrava*. Sells film rights to *Stick* for 350,000 dollars and to *LaBrava* for 400,000 dollars.

1984 *LaBrava* wins Edgar Allan Poe Award from Mystery Writers of America as Best Mystery Novel of the Year.

1985 *Glitz,* first novel to reach *New York Times* best-seller list. Is profiled in several national publications and appears on cover of *Newsweek*. Film version of *Stick* appears.

1986 Film version of *Fifty-Two Pickup* is released.

1987 *Bandits. Touch,* written ten years earlier, is also finally published.

1988 *Freaky Deaky*.

1

"Who Is Elmore Leonard?"

When Don Fine, head of Arbor House, sent him a copy of Elmore Leonard's *City Primeval* in 1980, John D. MacDonald asked, "Who is Elmore Leonard?" MacDonald wasn't alone; few had heard of this veteran writer even though he had already published sixteen novels prior to *City Primeval*. But the situation was about to change dramatically.

Just two years later, Ken Tucker wrote a *Village Voice* review that praised Leonard as "the finest thriller writer alive."[1] Two years after that, J. D. Reed, in an essay in *Time,* tabbed him "a Dickens from Detroit."[2] The following year Leonard graced the cover of *Newsweek* and in the accompanying article, Peter Prescott lauded him as "the best American writer of crime fiction alive, possibly the best we've ever had."[3]

And then just as quickly he was propelled out of genre fiction and into the center of the literary spotlight. In its 1987 "Guide to the Literary Universe," *Esquire* placed him in "The Red-Hot Center" in the select company of four other prominent American fiction writers: Saul Bellow, Raymond Carver, Norman Mailer, and John Updike. With dizzying speed, Leonard went from obscurity to fame to literary prominence. In his case, however, the phenomenon was certainly not a simple case of being just another "overnight success." It took Leonard over thirty years of hard work and dedication to his craft before an audience of critics and readers discovered just how good he was.

Elmore John Leonard, Jr., was born on October 11, 1925, in New Orleans, Louisiana, to Elmore John and Flora Rivé Leonard. His father was employed by General Motors as a scout for new dealership locations, and the family moved often in his early childhood: from New Orleans to Dallas to Oklahoma City, back to Dallas, then to Detroit for nine months, to Memphis and, in 1934, back to Detroit, where the family finally settled permanently.

As a youngster, Leonard attended Blessed Sacrament Elementary School in Detroit and then the Jesuit-run University of Detroit High School, where he benefited from the Jesuits' emphasis on the classics (four years of Latin, two of Greek) and from their insistence that he learn how to think for himself. No mere bookworm, he also played quarterback on the football team and was a pitcher on the baseball team. It was baseball, in fact, that inspired his nickname "Dutch"—he was named after the Washington Senators' knuckleball pitcher Dutch Leonard—and as the only Elmore for miles around, he recalls he desperately needed a nickname (which he still uses today).

Leonard's first writing experience came in the fifth grade. After reading a serialization of *All Quiet on the Western Front* in the local newpaper, he wrote a play about World War I trench warfare. In his drama, the hero is hung up on barbed wire (represented by the classroom desks) and must be rescued by the coward of the piece, who thus redeems himself.

Though he wrote one short story for his high-school paper, as a youth Leonard's artistic interests leaned more towards films than writing. He used to love to "tell movies" to his friends; he'd see a movie (*Captain Blood* and *Lives of a Bengal Lancer* were particular favorites) and re-create it scene by scene for his friends. At an early age he was thus displaying the kind of cinematic imagination he would later put to such good use in his fiction.

In the summer of 1943, Leonard attempted to join the marines, but was rejected because of a bad eye. Later that year, however, he was drafted and ended up in the navy. He served as a storekeeper's mate with the Seabees (construction battalions) in New Guinea and the Admiralty Islands where he recalls he passed out beer and emptied garbage. His official duties included helping to maintain an airstrip used by navy and Australian fighter planes. Like many other young sailors, his service experience also included the ritual tattooing: the name Dutch is tattooed in script on his left shoulder.

After the war, he returned home and in the fall of 1946 enrolled at the University of Detroit, where he majored in English and philosophy. Writing was still not a consuming passion ("I guess I was too busy reading to write"),[4] though he twice entered short-story contests sponsored by the Manuscribblers, a college creative writing club. He submitted one story (entitled "Kitchen Inquisition") because his English teacher promised a B grade to any student who did, and he needed a good grade to offset the D he received for a paper on Thackeray's *Vanity Fair*. He ended up somewhere in the top ten. His second entry was a story about a love triangle that he submitted when he was a senior. This time he finished second. The only other extracurricular writing he did were the book reports he wrote for a fellow student, Bill Marshall, now a Florida private eye. Marshall recalls that on one such assignment, he received two grades: an A for the writing, an F for the plagiarism.

In 1949, Leonard married Beverly Cline. The following year, after graduation from college, he took a job with the Campbell-Ewald Advertising Agency in Detroit. Two years earlier, his father had left General Motors to open an auto dealership in Las Cruces, New Mexico, with the idea that his son would join him in the business. His death six months after opening the agency put an end to that plan. It wouldn't have worked anyway because, Leonard admits, "I don't like cars."[5] And so he became an office boy for Campbell-Ewald ("I was their first married office boy").[6] Later, after leaving for a fifteen-month stint with a smaller agency, he returned to Campbell-Ewald as an advertising copywriter.

Leonard's specialty was ads for Chevrolet trucks. The agency liked his truck ads because he could make them sound gritty and tough. With cars you had to be cute and lyrical and use lots of imagery, similes, and metaphors and, as he confesses, "I've never been any good at similes and metaphors."[7] Though the agency liked his ads, they weren't yet ready for the blunt approach that would later become a hallmark of his dialogue: his proposal that a Chevy truck ad use one driver's straightforward endorsement—"You don't wear that sonofabitch out, you just get tired of looking at it and buy a new one"[8]—was rejected.

After college, a Detroit literary agent who had been a judge for one of the short-story contests Leonard entered invited him to join a local writers' club. At the time Leonard was reading such crime writers as Fredric Brown and Erle Stanley Gardner, especially the Bertha Cool-Donald Lam stories Gardner wrote under the name A. A. Fair. While a member of the group, Leonard wrote one story, a hard-boiled tale of revenge entitled "Seven Letter Word for Corpse."

Though up to this point in his life he had actually written only a couple of stories, Leonard made a critical decision. He had always loved reading, ever since his older sister Margaret ("Mickey") read to him regularly as a child. Writing itself had always come naturally to him and his lifelong love of movies had left him with a fascination for telling stories. So he decided to be a writer. Determining he couldn't afford to be a "literary" writer whose work ended up in the quarterlies, he picked a genre, westerns, for which there was a ready market in both slicks and pulp magazines. He had loved westerns since first seeing Gary Cooper's *The Plainsman* as a child. Besides, as he recalls, the western genre "wasn't exactly a field crowded with good writers."[9] It seemed a good place to learn.

He had no luck selling his first western story; it suffered, he was forced to conclude, from a lack of authenticity. Though he was a fan of western movies and an occasional reader of such western writers as Luke Short, Ernest Haycox, and James Warner Bellah, he actually knew very little about the west. So, as he would continue to do throughout his career, he began researching his subject. He read *Arizona Highways* magazine, which gave him pictorial information about the look of the west; in addition it contained serious essays about a variety of western subjects. He also read gun catalogs and books about the Apaches and the US cavalry.

He also sat down and began carefully studying Ernest Hemingway's fiction, especially *For Whom the Bell Tolls*. Long an admirer of Hemingway's work, Leonard now read it with an eye to learning from Hemingway's example. He would analyze how Hemingway approached a scene, how he used point of view, how he revealed so much simply by the way a character talked, and how he made the words he used count. He would open up Hemingway's novel of the Spanish Civil War anywhere "just to get the feel of it, just get in the mood of it."[10] *For Whom the Bell Tolls* taught him how to write westerns "because I saw it as a kind of western."[11] (One of Leonard's prized possessions is an autographed photograph of Hemingway given to him by a Miami lawyer, which hangs prominently above the desk in his office where he writes.)

One thing Leonard did not derive from Hemingway, however, was his attitude. "It didn't take too long to see that my attitude was different from his. I see more absurdity. I like people more. I'm more tolerant."[12] So while he learned many of his fictional techniques from Hemingway, his outlook on life was influenced much more by such popular writers of the day as Richard Bissell, Mark Harris, and Kurt Vonnegut, Jr. who, like him, were more inclined to recognize the absurdities in life than was Hemingway.

The first story Leonard wrote after his research into the west was titled "Tizwin" (the name for Apache corn beer). He sent it to *Argosy,* which rejected it; however, the editor sent him an encouraging letter and also forwarded the story to Mike Tilden, editor of several western pulps. (Tilden later purchased it and published it as "Red Hell Hits Canyon Diablo" in the October 1952 issue of *10 Story Western*). Greatly encouraged, Leonard sent another story to *Argosy,* a twelve-thousand–word novelette entitled "Apache Agent." John Bender, the editor who read it, liked it and offered Leonard a thousand dollars for it.

To a twenty-five-year-old unpublished writer with a wife, a one-year-old daughter and another child on the way, who was at the time making only $275 a month, the offer was a godsend. When the story, retitled "Trail of the Apache," appeared in the December 1951 issue of *Argosy,* it also led to his getting an agent. Marguerite Harper, a New York literary agent who numbered among her clients such well-known western writers as Luke Short and Peter

Dawson, wrote Leonard and offered her services as his agent. He gladly accepted.

Shortly thereafter, Marguerite sold "The Colonel's Lady" to *Zane Grey's Western* for $110. Two months later, she sold a second story to *Zane Grey's Western*, "Cavalry Boots," for $100. A few weeks after that, she sold "You Never See Apaches" to *Dime Western* for $100. By the end of 1952, she had sold nine of Leonard's western tales to the two-cents-a-word pulp market. The following year, she also sold the first of his novels, *The Bounty Hunters*, to Houghton-Mifflin for $3,000.

After his first half-dozen or so sales, Leonard decided that if he was ever going to produce anything but short stories, he needed more time to write. However, with a full-time job and with two young children at home, finding a good time to write wasn't easy. He tried writing in the evenings after work, but quickly found out he wasn't a night person. So he embarked on a spartan regimen of rising each morning at 5 A.M. and writing until 7 A.M., when he would leave for work.

He set a rule for himself that he couldn't even heat the water for coffee (even in the cold Michigan winter mornings) until he had written at least a paragraph. He wanted to avoid any excuse for delaying work. His goal was to write two pages a day before he had to leave for his job at Campbell-Ewald. "It was a chore," he readily admits, "but I knew that's what I had to do."[13] Later at work he would occasionally continue writing on a yellow legal pad he kept hidden in his desk drawer; whenever he'd spot someone approaching his office, he'd quietly close the drawer.

Marguerite Harper offered constant encouragement and prodding. Her aim was to get his work accepted by the more prestigious (and better-paying) magazines like *Saturday Evening Post* and *Collier's*. (She eventually achieved her goal by selling one story, "Moment of Vengeance" to the *Post* in 1955. The *Post* editors usually complained that his fiction was too gray, too relentless, without enough romantic or comic interest.) Mindful of the hazards of the writing profession, Marguerite also on more than one occasion warned her young client not to give up his job. The second letter she ever wrote him contained in bold print the stern warning, "Don't Give up Your Job to Write." And so for the next several years he continued rising at 5 A.M. to write fiction before going off to crank out Chevy ads.

Leonard's determination and hard work eventually paid off. By the end of the decade, he had managed to make a name for himself as a western writer. He had published four novels: *The Bounty Hunters* (1953), *The Law at Randado* (1954), *Escape from Five Shadows* (1956), and *Last Stand at Saber River* (1959). In addition, he had sold one story to the *Saturday Evening Post,* four to *Argosy,* and at least twenty-three more to virtually every important western pulp on the market: *Zane Grey's Western, Dime Western, 10-Story Western, Western Story Magazine, Gunsmoke, Fifteen Western Tales, Western Story Roundup, Western Magazine, Western Story Magazine, Complete Western Book, 2-Gun Western, Western Short Stories,* and *Western Novel and Short Stories.*

His stories were also beginning to be reprinted regularly in collections of western tales and some were also being purchased by Hollywood: his 1953 *Dime Western* story, "Three-Ten to Yuma," was sold to Columbia Pictures and made into a 1957 film, *3:10 to Yuma,* starring Van Heflin and Glenn Ford; "The Captives," which appeared in *Argosy* in February 1955, was also bought by Columbia and made into *The Tall T* (also released in 1957), with Randolph Scott and Richard Boone. In addition, his *Saturday Evening Post* story, "Moment of Vengeance," was sold to television's *Schlitz Playhouse.*

Unfortunately, at about the same time he established his reputation as a western writer, the western market began to dry up. Westerns were still popular, but mainly on television. In 1959, for example, there were thirty prime-time western series on television. This was the same year Leonard wrote one of his best westerns, *Hombre,* but because of the decline in the publication market it took more than two years to sell the novel. And then he received only $1,250 for it, barely more than he had earned for his first story in 1951. It was time to try something else.

When Leonard's profit-sharing plan with Campbell-Ewald came due in 1961, he decided to take the money, quit his job, and become a full-time fiction writer. This was a risky proposition for a man who now had four kids to support and whose established fiction market had all but disappeared. The next five years turned out to be the low point in his career, for he published nothing. To support his family, he was forced to do free-lance writing. He opened his own advertising agency and worked on ad accounts for Chevy, Avon Chemical, and Hurst Shifters. He also wrote a number of industrial and educational films: he turned out a dozen short films for Encyclopedia Brittanica Films on such subjects as Julius Caesar, The French and Indian Wars, and the settling of the Mississippi Valley, for which he received a thousand dollars each. Writing slogans for elephant blankets (which he did) and recruiting films for the Franciscans (which he also did) was not exactly what he had in mind when he left Campbell-Ewald with the dream of becoming a full-time writer.

Then in 1965, Twentieth Century-Fox purchased film rights to *Hombre* for ten thousand dollars, which enabled him to quit his free-lance activities (except for one account, which he kept to help pay the bills) and begin working seriously on a new novel. But with the western market gone, he knew he had to try something different. He had never especially enjoyed writing westerns anyway. ("What the hell am I doing writing westerns?" he once asked himself; "I don't even like the period.")[14] Also, with westerns he never felt he was using everything he knew: "I was in second gear; I wasn't using what was going on around me."[15] So he set out to write a novel set in contemporary Michigan with the title, *Mother, This Is Jack Ryan.*

Shortly after he sent Marguerite Harper the completed manuscript of the novel in 1966, she became seriously ill. She forwarded it on to H. N. Swanson, the Hollywood agent who had been handling Leonard's movie sales. Swanson is an almost-legendary figure whose list of clients reads like a *Who's Who of Twentieth-Century American Literature:* Ernest Hemingway. F. Scott Fitzgerald, William Faulkner, Raymond Chandler, James M. Cain, John O'Hara, Cornell Woolrich, Nathanael West. When Swanson read the manuscript of *Mother, This Is Jack Ryan,* he phoned Leonard and asked him if he really wrote it. When Leonard replied of course he did, Swanson promised, "Kiddo, I'm going to make you rich."[16]

Swanson began sending the manuscript to publishers and movie studios in 1966. Within three months, he had amassed a total of eighty-four rejections. Refusing to be discouraged by this response, Leonard went to work revising the novel. His new version, retitled *The Big Bounce,* finally met with success: Swanson sold it both to Fawcett Books, which brought it out as a paperback original in 1969, and to Warner Brothers, which released it as a film the same year with Ryan O'Neal and Leigh Taylor-Young. Though the film was in Leonard's estimation perhaps the worst movie ever made (he claims to have walked out of the theater after watching only twenty minutes of it), the publication of his first nonwestern novel opened new doors for him.

Up to this point Leonard had achieved moderate success in selling his works to Hollywood; now he tried selling himself as a screenplay writer. The first screenplay he sold was based on a Prohibition-era novel of his entitled *The Moonshine War,* published by Doubleday in 1969. (The film, directed by Richard Quine and starring Richard Widmark and Alan Alda, was released in 1970.) Swanson was so impressed with the script he promised Leonard that if he ever decided he wanted a career as a film writer, he was ready to back him.

In the early 1970s, Leonard sold several more screenplays to Hollywood studios, though only two films were ever actually produced from these scripts: *Joe Kidd,* a 1972 Universal release starring Clint Eastwood, and *Mr. Majestyk,* a Charles Bronson film released by United Artists in 1974. During this period he also wrote two more paperback westerns—one, *Valdez Is Coming* (1970), for Fawcett, the other, *Forty Lashes Less One* (1972), for Bantam—plus a novel based on his *Mr. Majestyk* screenplay, which came out as a Dell paperback in 1974.

In 1972, Swanson suggested that he read *The Friends of Eddie Coyle,* a debut novel just published by George V. Higgins about a small-time Boston hood. Leonard was enormously impressed by Higgins's method of telling his story. "I became more mature as a writer after I read Higgins," he acknowledges. "I learned to just relax and tell the story. His casual use of obscenities and 'true' dialogue impressed me."[17] From Higgins he also learned that you could "just jump into a scene from somebody's point of view. Nobody cares what the writer thinks." (When the *Washington Post* asked several writers in 1986 to pick their favorite books, Leonard's choice was *The Friends of Eddie Coyle.* "I can open [it] right now to any page," he wrote, "and say, that's it, yeah, that's how you do it.")[18]

Leonard's next novel, *Fifty-Two Pickup,* published in 1974, was a major turning point in his career. It was the first of his books written after he read George Higgins. It was also the first of his novels to be set in his hometown, which presented him with a new problem. With westerns, a photograph of a canyon or a mesa was all he needed to create a convincing backdrop for the action. With a place like Detroit, where readers actually lived who knew the streets and locations he would be using, the situation was different. How was he going to insure the accuracy of his descriptions?

Then he discovered that the key to description was to do it from somebody else's point of view and leave himself out of it. "I started to realize that the way to describe anywhere, *anywhere,* was to do it from someone's point of view," he said, "and *leave me out of it.* I'm not gonna get poetic about this street," he decided. "That's not what I do."[19] It was much more effective, he found, to have one of his characters say it's a lousy day than to have to describe the day himself.

Thus was born what Leonard has described as his "sound," which is, more accurately, the sound of his characters rather than the sound of his voice. This led to a related discovery: i.e., that his characters didn't have to be conventional heroes, that like Higgins he could have fun with colorful characters who live outside the law.

The mid-1970s was a period of dramatic change in Leonard's life. Professionally, he was beginning to enjoy moderate success, making a living as a writer of screenplays and novels. More importantly, he was finding his narrative voice and discovering the appropriate subject for his fiction. But while his career was on the rise, his personal life headed into a tailspin. In 1974, he left his wife of twenty-five years and five children and moved into a nearby apartment. And he joined Alcoholics Anonymous.

Like many other noted American authors (including some of Swanson's famous clients: Hemingway, Fitzgerald, Faulkner, Woolrich), Leonard developed a serious problem with alcohol. "For twenty years I was a happy drunk. Then," he confesses, "I started to get wild."[20] In a revealing autobiographical essay included in Dennis Wholey's *The Courage to Change: Hope and Help for Alcoholics—and Their Families,* Leonard recalls his days as a heavy drinker. In the service, he routinely drank six to eight cans of beer a day. At Campbell-Ewald, he felt the need for a drink whenever he met with clients. On his own after leaving Campbell-Ewald, he would wait until noon, then begin drinking.

By the early 1970s, his drinking got worse. Returning home to Detroit from a meeting in Hollywood one day, he was hospitalized when he started vomiting blood. His doctor assured him he was probably suffering from an ulcer rather than acute gastritis, which he said was usually only found in skid-row bums. When they opened him up, they discovered he had acute gastritis.

He also now began getting arrested for drunk driving. In 1974, at the urging of some friends, he agreed to start attending Alcoholics Anonymous meetings. For the next three years, he would quit drinking periodically, only to resume again after a few months. Finally in 1977, with the encouragement of Joan Shepard, whom he met during his separation from his wife (and who in 1979 would become his second wife), he succeeded in quitting entirely; at 9 A.M.

on January 24, 1977, he had his last drink ("I think it was Scotch and ginger ale").[21]

"I didn't end up in the weeds," Leonard acknowledges, though he came to realize he was drinking too much. "I might put the first drink off till noon, but I needed alcohol to get me going."[22] Though he never drank anything like a couple of fifths a day, what he did drink became a problem because it changed his personality and behavior, turning him into an uncharacteristically loud and boisterous person. He insists his drinking never interfered with his work, that he knew enough never to drink while writing, only afterwards. But he also acknowledges that both his writing and his personal relationships have improved since he stopped. Among other things, he admits to liking his characters more, "probably because I like myself more."[23]

By the end of the 1970s, things were looking up for Leonard: he had won his battle with booze; he had remarried; he continued to turn out a steady stream of novels: *Swag* (1976), *The Hunted* (1977), *Unknown Man No. 89* (1977), *The Switch* (1978), *Gunsights* (1979), and *Gold Coast* (1980). He also accepted a writing assignment that would result in a new richness and authenticity in his writing.

In 1978, the *Detroit News* asked Leonard to write a feature article for their Sunday magazine about the Detroit police. He originally planned to spend a few days hanging around police headquarters at 1300 Beaubien in downtown Detroit. Once there, however, his attitude quickly changed. "Oh my God," he realized, "this is too good!"[24] Instead of staying a few days, he remained for two-and-a-half months, listening to the cops and criminals, lawyers and witnesses who filed through the homicide squad room, soaking up their colorful language and distinctive speech rhythms. His article, "Impressions of Murder," which appeared in the November 12, 1978, issue of the paper, paints a vivid picture of real policemen at work.

Though Leonard did not follow up this assignment with any more nonfiction pieces, his lengthy exposure to the police proved to have a significant impact on his subsequent fiction. While the novels written prior to this experience were already convincingly realistic, those written afterwards, beginning with *City Primeval,* published in 1980, were marked by a new grittiness and pungency.

Leonard's subsequent fiction has also benefited from two other research resources. In 1977, after an absence of some twenty-five years, Leonard contacted an old college chum named Bill Marshall, whom he had learned from mutual friends was now a private eye in Coral Gables, Florida. Leonard was thinking about setting a book in Florida, a state he had been visiting for years, and needed some help. He called Marshall and reminded him he still owed him for all those book reports he wrote for him while both were students at the University of Detroit. The two rekindled their friendship and Marshall assisted in the research not only for *Gold Coast,* the first of Leonard's books set in Florida, but also for the four additional novels he eventually set in the Sunshine State.

Leonard met Gregg Sutter, director of research for a Detroit firm, and a longtime fan, for the first time in 1979. Sutter interviewed Leonard several times for a profile he wrote that appeared in the August 1980 issue of *Monthly Detroit* magazine, the first such in-depth piece on Leonard to appear. A few months later, in January 1981, Leonard called Sutter and asked him if he'd like to do some research for him on his new novel, *Split Images*. Sutter jumped at the chance and has been Leonard's researcher ever since.

In 1986, Sutter published an informative two-part essay in *The Armchair Detective* detailing his behind-the-scenes contribution to Leonard's fiction. He describes how he provides Leonard whatever he needs—photographs, documents, names, library materials, even location research—and then watches as Leonard takes the bits and pieces he's given, uses what he needs, and transforms the raw material into his fiction. Though Sutter modestly likens his role to that of "Mickey Mantle's batboy,"[25] like the Detroit police at 1300 Beaubien he too has made an important contribution to the richer texture that has characterized Leonard's post-1980 fiction.

Despite his modest success, by 1980 Leonard was still largely a well-kept secret. His novels weren't being widely reviewed, though when they were they usually received highly favorable notices. The pseudonymous Newgate Callendar of the *New York Times,* for example, was one of the first to recognize Leonard's talent: as early as 1974, in a review of *Fifty-Two Pickup,* he praised Leonard as "a very good writer"; two years later, he called *Swag* "one of the best of the year" and said it "will have the critics mentioning Chandler and Higgins—it's that good";[26] then in 1977, in a review of *Unknown Man No. 89,* he enthusiastically proclaimed the arrival of "a new and important writer of mystery fiction," who can "write circles around almost anybody active in the crime novel today."[27] And he wasn't alone. In her review of *Unknown Man No. 89* for *Cosmopolitan,* Jane Clapperton called Leonard "an immensely gifted writer."[28]

But if it weren't for his movie work, both the screenplays he was writing and the profitable sales of the film rights to his novels, Leonard would have had to resume free-lance advertising work. (Because he needed the fifty thousand dollars CBS offered, he even agreed in 1980 to the dubious project of writing the script for the television movie sequel to *High Noon* entitled *High Noon, Part II: The Return of Will Kane.*) He was growing increasingly frustrated with his publishers' inability to market his works successfully. "They'd try to sell me as 'the new Hammett' or 'the new Chandler,'" he complained. "I'd say don't sell Hammett. Hell, I've never even read Hammett. Sell Leonard."[29]

Part of the problem was that his books didn't have a continuing character. Also, his main characters were car thieves, con men, and small-time hoods, not the sort of heroes usually found in popular fiction. Neither of his publishers—first Delacorte, then Bantam—could quite figure out how to promote him successfully. Delacorte tried to sell *Unknown Man No. 89* as a Raymond Chandler–type novel by using the line, "Imagine Philip Marlowe serving a summons in Detroit." Worse still, they promoted the novel as Jack Ryan's third appearance, when he actually appeared only once before. His own publishers confused him with Frank Ryan of *Swag.*

Bantam was so uncertain about what to do with *Touch,* written in 1978, that it decided at the last minute not to publish the novel at all, even though it was already set into type. Because of their delay, Bantam later lost publishing rights to the novel, for which it had paid $30,000; several years later Leonard resold the rights to *Touch* to Arbor House for $300,000 and it finally appeared in 1987.

In 1980, Don Fine, who had been his editor at Dell in the 1950s, started a new publishing company, Arbor House, and sought to sign Leonard. "I'll pay you less than what you've been getting," he told him, "but I'll get across to readers and reviewers how good you are. We'll create a whole Elmore Leonard reputation."[30] Leonard accepted his offer, and *City Primeval* became the first of his novels to come out under the Arbor House imprint. True to his word, Fine got the book into the right hands. He even used John D. MacDonald's "Who is Elmore Leonard?" comment in the promotion for the book, as well as MacDonald's highly flattering subsequent endorsement: "Leonard can really write. He is astonishingly good. He doesn't cheat the reader. He gives full value."

City Primeval was followed by four novels in quick succession: *Split Images* (1981), *Cat Chaser* (1982), *Stick,* and *LaBrava* (both 1983). The secret was getting out and the chorus of critical praise from reviewers who suddenly "discovered" Leonard was growing louder and louder. The *New Yorker* in its review of *Cat Chaser* praised Leonard as "a gripping writer—a really first-rate writer";[31] Michele Slung, reviewing the novel for the *Washington Post,* commented, "Rarely have I felt in such capable authorial hands."[32] Reviewers abroad were also discovering Leonard. Allan Jones, in a review that appeared in a British publication called *Melody Maker,* concluded: "Elmore Leonard's books are object lessons in the art of fine writing. I can think of few other authors who write with such lean precision, such blistering, uncluttered narrative pace, such disciplined economy. . . . Leonard can write the lapels off virtually every other thriller writer on the shelves."[33]

Stick also earned rave reviews by important critics. Jonathan Yardley in the *Washington Post* proclaimed, "Leonard is the real thing. . . . He raises the hard-boiled suspense novel beyond the limits of genre and into social commentary";[34] George Stade in the *New York Times* wrote, "He gives us as much serious fun per word as anyone around."[35] Neal Johnston in the *New York Times Book Review* praised *LaBrava* for being "about as good as the form allows."[36] The selection of that novel as winner of the Edgar Allan Poe Award from the Mystery Writers of America as the Best Novel of 1984 also brought him new attention.

As his books began to receive such high praise, Leonard became something of a celebrity. In December of 1984, he was profiled in both *GQ* (by Pulitzer-prize winning writer J. Anthony Lukas) and the *New York Times Magazine*. Then with the publication of *Glitz* in early 1985, Leonard became the hottest writer in America: he was profiled in *Rolling Stone* and *People Magazine;* his picture appeared on the cover of *Newsweek;* he was invited to appear on the "Phil Donahue Show"; George Will devoted his nationally syndicated column to him; Pete Hamill wrote about him in the *New York Daily News Magazine; Chicago Tribune* columnist Bob Greene devoted not one but two columns to his work. And for the first time one of his books reached the *New York Times* best-seller list.

His next novel, *Bandits,* fared just as well, becoming another national best-seller. And Leonard continued to enjoy the benefits of his new fame. His photograph was featured prominently in a series of advertisements for American Express that appeared in several national magazines in 1987. Also worthy of note was his selection in 1987 by *Playgirl* magazine as one of the Ten Sexiest Men of the Year. (Informed of the honor, Leonard wondered exactly what year that was!)

With critical acclaim also came unprecedented financial rewards. For example, after *Glitz,* Arbor House had to shell out $3 million for his next two novels, *Bandits* and *Freaky Deaky*. Another measure of his skyrocketing popularity were the sums paid for paperback rights to his books: *Split Images* sold for a modest $7,000; *Cat Chaser* for $10,000; *Stick* brought $50,000; *La Brava* went for $363,000; *Glitz* for a staggering $450,000. Hollywood, too, now had to pay the price for Leonard's new popularity: he received $350,000 for the film rights and screenplay to *Stick*, $400,000 for *La Brava*, $450,000 for *Glitz*. After over three decades of hard work and relative obscurity, Leonard had made it and made it big.

Leonard's reaction to his elevated status was a mixture of bewilderment and bemusement. Things were suddenly going so well, he joked, that "these days . . . I could sell my letters to my mother."[37] He confessed to being happy about *Glitz* making the best-seller lists, but added, "I hope to God I never take it too seriously."[38] What astonished him about the entire phenomenon was the knowledge that he wasn't doing anything differently. In his opinion, the success of *Glitz* was more a matter of timing than writing: the momentum that had been building ever since he joined Arbor House in 1980 had suddenly achieved its purpose and was now paying impressive dividends.

Though widespread popularity and critical acclaim came late, success came on his terms: he was never forced to compromise his writing in any way. "What's most satisfying," he admits, "is that I've persisted in developing my way of writing. . . . I wrote exactly how I wanted to write. Now I have readers."[39] When asked why it took him so long to catch on, he replies it didn't take *him* that long, it took reviewers and readers that long to catch up with him. "Reviewers wonder where I've been," he said. "Only a few wonder where they've been."[40]

When questioned how it feels to have achieved success so late in his career, he responds, with justifiable pride, that he has always considered himself successful as a writer: "A lot of people see me sitting in a cold basement in my overcoat, writing, hoping that someday there'll be a breakthrough," he notes. "But I've always done very well. It never occurred to me during all those years that I wasn't successful."[41] Most everything he wrote was published, he had a small but loyal core of readers, and the bulk of his work was sold to Hollywood.

Success certainly hasn't slowed him down any. In fact, today he's working as hard as ever. In addition to his novels, he continues to write screenplays (two of which appeared in 1987: *The Rosary Murders,* a film based on fellow Detroit author William Kienzle's novel, and *Desperado,* a western film that was telecast on NBC.) And he continues to talk with various producers and networks about possible television series.

Because fame and fortune came so late in his career (he didn't have his first best-seller until he was fifty-nine), his life has changed very little. He and his wife Joan still live quietly in Birmingham, Michigan, their seven children (five of his and two of hers) and five grandchildren nearby. He continues to write from 9:30 to 6:00 almost every day at the same two-hundred-year-old writing desk he has owned for years. He still composes on specially ordered unlined yellow paper of heavy stock with a favorite pen: "I feel so much closer to the material with a pen," he admits. "That, to me, is writing."[42]

Leonard composes in longhand, then crosses out, then writes some more. "If it looks like *writing,*" he says, "I rewrite it."[43] Usually, he ends up crossing out more than he keeps. "It gets pretty messy," he admits. "I can barely read the pages when I'm done."[44] When he is finally satisfied with the work, he types it himself on a reconditioned Olympic typewriter, occasionally making additional changes as he types.

At the end of the day, Leonard will often read what he has written aloud to his wife to get her reaction. He credits Joan with having an unerring instinct when something's wrong, for example when a character is behaving out of character, or when he's using too many words. "Joan doesn't necessarily have to put her finger specifically on it," he says, "but invariably there is something wrong."[45]

What if by some stroke of misfortune, all the critical acclaim and popular acceptance were suddenly to disappear and he found himself with no more readers than he had in those days of literary obscurity? It wouldn't make any difference in his life, he says. "My satisfaction is in doing the work, performing, not taking bows,"[46] he insists. "I'd still write. It's what I do."[47]

2

Apache Apprenticeship

Deciding to write westerns as a way of launching a literary career was not a difficult choice for Leonard, even though he lived in the industrial North and had never actually been in the west. He hoped to become a commercially successful writer and in the early 1950s there still existed a ready market for western stories. Besides, as a longtime fan of western films, Leonard had a feel for the characters and conventions of the western genre.

What he didn't know about the west (which was plenty) he learned by doing careful research. In addition to studying the pictures and articles in *Arizona Highways* magazine, he read gun magazines and catalogs as well as such books as *The Look of the Old West,* by Foster Harris. Once he decided to specialize in Apaches, he also read John C. Cremony's *Life among the Apaches,* Frank C. Lockwood's *The Apache Indians,* and two volumes by Morris Edward Opler, *An Apache Life-Way* and *Myths and Tales of The Chiricahua Apache Indians.* Leonard soon developed a feel for the Southwest as well as a specialized knowledge of the Apache way of life that added a convincing element of authenticity to the stories he would write.

Leonard's first published story, "Trail of the Apache" (*Argosy,* 1951), is an action-packed cowboys-and-Indians adventure tale set in 1880. Sixteen hostile Apaches are delivered into the custody of Captain Eric Travisin, head of the Apache agency at Camp Gila, Arizona, a man with a reputation for success in pacifying Apaches. One night, the Indians escape. The following day, Travisin has to lead a contingent of men across the sun-scorched Arizona desert after them.

The story is peopled with the usual assortment of stock characters: Travisin, the savvy, experienced Apache agent; deBoth, the pink-cheeked young army lieutenant who has yet to prove himself under fire; and Pillo, the proud and fiery leader of the renegade Apaches. Rather than subtlety of characterization, Leonard relies on plenty of action and the excitement of the pursuit, all played out against the colorful Arizona background (largely constructed from pictures in magazines).

Though "Trail of the Apache" provides early evidence of Leonard's skill in handling dramatic action, it also reveals his lack of confidence in allowing the action itself to carry the story. At times he pumps exitement into his scenes by resorting to overheated language and images. For example, he describes one Apache assault with this overripe simile: they came "screaming down the passage like a cloud of vampires beating from a cavern."[1] The final bloody battle in the story is presented in similarly melodramatic language: "Savage closed with savage in a grinding melee of thrashing arms and legs in thick dust, the cornered animal, made more ferocious by his fear, battling the hunter who had tasted blood."[2]

Despite its flaws, "Trail of the Apache" showed that Leonard could write a convincing story and hold the reader's attention. Not wanting to abandon a successful formula, he quickly turned out several more tales that featured Apaches and the cavalry in one way or another. In stories with titles like "Apache Medicine," "You Never See Apaches" (both *Dime Western,* 1952), and "Red Hell Hits Canyon Diablo" (*10 Story Western,* 1952), whose original title, "Tizwin" (the name for Apache corn beer), was changed by the editors, Leonard played variations on the Apache-cavalry formula.

After a half-dozen stories, Leonard put aside the colorful Apache material and began to concentrate more on character and situation. "The Rustlers" (*Zane Grey's Western,* 1953), for example, tells the story of Emmett Ryan, who is charged with the task of capturing the rustlers who stole a hundred head of cattle from his employer. The story focuses less on Ryan's pursuit of the rustlers than on his moral dilemma when he finally catches up with them: one of the horse thieves is his brother Jack and the standard penalty for rustling is hanging; will Ryan turn his brother in?

Leonard's first major success was "Three-Ten to Yuma" (*Dime Western,* 1953), the first of his works to be sold to Hollywood. (It was made into a memorable 1957 film directed by Delmer Daves and starring Van Heflin and Glenn Ford.) Marshall Paul Scallen is charged with the responsibility of placing his prisoner, Jim Kidd, safely on the 3:10 train to Yuma. The two hole up in a hotel room at dawn and begin the tense wait for the afternoon train to arrive. Meanwhile, seven of Kidd's henchmen gather in town and camp outside the hotel, ready to spring Kidd when Scallen attempts to put him on the train.

The story, obviously indebted to *High Noon,* which was released in 1952, reveals Leonard's growing interest in suspense over action. The question of whether or not Scallen will prevail against seven-to-one odds is of course important, but it is the way Scallen reacts to the situation that interests Leonard as much as the outcome. While there is, not surprisingly, some gunplay in this story (and in the ones to follow), Leonard was beginning to show more and more interest in the man behind the gun rather than in the actions of the gun itself.

Another of Leonard's early stories, "The Captives" (*Argosy,* 1955), was also sold to Hollywood. (Directed by Budd Boetticher, the film, starring Randolph Scott and Richard Boone and retitled *The Tall T,* was released in 1957, the same year *3:10 to Yuma* hit the screen.) A trio of bandits robs a stage; during the holdup, one of the passengers, to save his skin, informs the outlaws that his wife is the daughter of a wealthy man who will pay plenty for her safe return. A ransom message is sent to the woman's father. Meanwhile, another one of the passengers tries to figure a way out of the situation, for he knows the bandits will surely kill them all. The characters are believable, the situation fraught with tension, and the resolution worked out in dramatic fashion.

If a western can be called hard-boiled, then Leonard's "Law of the

Hunted Ones" (*Western Story Magazine,* 1952) is a good example. The story opens with Virgil Patman and his young sidekick Dave Fallis riding off to find new jobs in Texas after being mustered out of the army. Along the way they stumble onto the hideout of two men, one of whom, Lew De Sana, is a prison escapee Patman once guarded. De Sana suspects that Patman is tracking him and invites his two "guests" to spend the night. This uneasy situation is further intensified, in the manner of James M. Cain, by the presence of a young woman, De Sana's girlfriend, whose bruised face bears evidence of her mistreatment by De Sana. She inevitably attracts Fallis's eye. The tension is then further increased by the arrival of a group of Apaches who are themselves after De Sana, who was serving time for murdering an Apache.

Leonard displays a sure hand in manipulating suspense by employing a narrative technique he would later use extensively in his crime fiction: he skillfully shifts the point of view from one character to another—from Patman to Fallis to De Sana, even to one of the approaching Apaches. The action unfolds unhurriedly, enabling the tension to build gradually. Tough characters, a dramatic situation, and straightforward presentation of the action combine to make "Law of the Hunted Ones" one of the grittiest of Leonard's western tales.

Many of Leonard's western stories are revenge tales. In "The Big Hunt" (*Western Story Magazine,* 1953), for example, a young man is cheated out of 480 buffalo skins by the same man who cheated his father four years earlier and then indirectly caused his death in a buffalo stampede. The youth gets his skins back and his revenge by triggering a stampede that destroys the camp of the man who had cheated both him and his father. In "The Boy Who Smiled" (*Gunsmoke,* 1953), a young half-breed Apache gets his revenge on those responsible for hanging his father for stealing a horse they knew he had obtained legally. He takes a job as guide to the pair of killers, leads them into the desert, shoots holes in their water bags, and then leaves them there to die. In "Man with the Iron Arm" (*Complete Western Book,* 1956), a one-armed man patiently waits several months until he gets the opportunity to pay back the man who had humiliated him because of his missing arm.

In these stories, satisfaction at achieving revenge is of less interest to Leonard than what achieving revenge reveals about the man who obtains it. In each instance the man who gains his revenge is initially underestimated by his opponent. The quiet man who surprises his opponent by displaying unsuspected courage would become a familiar Elmore Leonard character.

Leonard's agent, Marguerite Harper, kept trying to sell his stories to slick magazines like *Collier's* and the *Saturday Evening Post* because they paid much better than the pulps. She met with success only once, when the *Saturday Evening Post* purchased "Moment of Vengeance" and published it in 1956. The *Post* rejected the rest of Leonard's submissions, complaining that his stories lacked any romantic or comic relief. Leonard says a friend once jokingly told him, "Don't you know that to sell to the *Post,* you have to have Guy Kibbee in your story."[3] Rather than alter what he was doing in order to get his work accepted by magazines like the *Post,* he wisely chose to continue writing the kind of realistic westerns he had been doing; he resisted any suggestions that he lighten them up with comic or romantic relief to meet the requirements of any specific magazine.

Though invariably readable, Leonard's pulp tales break no new ground: characters, settings, and situations are all pretty much standard. Leonard was more interested in learning his craft than in being an innovator within the genre. However, his stories occasionally show evidence of experimenting a little, of trying new things, especially with point of view, as he was gradually developing his own fictional approach.

Leonard first moved beyond the pulps with the publication of his debut novel, *The Bounty Hunters,* which Houghton Mifflin published in 1953. Once again he drew upon the familiar subject of Apaches and cavalrymen for his material. The novel form provided him with a much larger canvas than he was used to in his short stories, although in taking advantage of the additional space he ended up with a book as crowded with figures as a Brueghel painting.

Cavalry scout Dave Flynn is assigned to accompany a young army lieutenant, Duane Bowers, on a mission to Mexico to return Soldado Viejo, a hostile Mimbre Apache chief, to the Apache Agency in Arizona. En route, the two come upon the ruins of a wagon train; men, women, and children, all members of a Mexican family Flynn knew, have been murdered and scalped in what is designed to look like an Apache raid.

Flynn, however, is too schooled in Apache ways to fall for the deceit. It turns out he is right, for he later learns that those responsible for the slaughter were a gang of outlaws led by Frank Lazair. Lazair has been earning a hundred pesos for each Apache scalp he turns over to Lamas Duro, head of the *rurales,* the Mexican border police. Duro knows the latest batch of scalps didn't come from Apaches, but since he pockets ten pesos for every hundred he pays out, he isn't about to make a fuss.

At this point the reader might find a scorecard useful. In addition to Lazair and his fourteen men and Duro and his battalion of *rurales,* Soldado Viejo and his tribe of Apaches also figure prominently in the action (Lazair has been killing Apache women and old men and selling their scalps to Duro). Into this already percolating situation Leonard adds two additional elements: Frank Rellis, who tangled (and lost) with Flynn and his buddy Joe Madora in a dispute at the beginning of the book, later shot Madora and fled; when Flynn shows up in Mexico, who should spot him but Rellis, who is now one of Lazair's scalp hunters. Also, the sole survivor of the slaughter of the wagon train, Nita Esteban, has been taken captive by Lazair; her father, a friend of Flynn's, asks his help in getting her back.

Employing a solution he would later put to good use in several of his crime novels, Leonard has Flynn come up with a plan that pits the various factions against one another. Eventually, the villains are all killed and the three cavalry men—Flynn, Bowers, and the wounded Joe Madora who later joins them—emerge as winners.

There is no lack of action in the novel and, as is the case with most of Leonard's early stories, action takes precedence over character. The characters are distinctly drawn, though they remain rather one-dimensional figures. The good guys—Flynn, Bowers, Madora, Esteban—are purely good guys, while the villains—Lazair, Duro, and Frank Rellis—are stereotypical bad guys. And in true western morality-play fashion, good triumphs over evil.

The Bounty Hunters includes a scene in which Flynn and Soldado have a face-to-face encounter. Though antagonists, the two men have come to respect each other: Soldado didn't get to be an old man without intelligence and wisdom; and as a veteran of ten years as a cavalry scout, Flynn has learned to appreciate the Apache ways and never to underestimate his opponents. Flynn tries to convince Soldado that he cannot escape the inevitable victory of the white man. "It is only foolish when you fight against what is bound to happen,"[4] he counsels. If Soldado refuses to return to the reservation, he will be hunted down and imprisoned. "What is the difference in meaning between these words prison and reservation?"[5] Soldado asks.

The scene is typical of Leonard's western fiction in its sympathetic portrayal of the Apaches. Though often used to provide impetus for the plot, the Apaches are never presented simply as screaming, bloodthirsty savages, never used simply as embodiments of the evil the good guys must battle. Individual Apaches are sometimes portrayed as killers, but they are always shown as exceptions rather than the rule. The Apaches' plight as a proud people forced to surrender their freedom and their land and submit to reservation life under the jurisdiction of the US Army is never downplayed in Leonard's fiction.

Leonard's second novel, *The Law at Randado* (1954), suffers from the opposite problem that plagued *The Bounty Hunters:* instead of an excess of action, this novel suffers from a lack of it, or at least the lack of unified action. The novel reads like two separate stories linked rather tenuously together.

The book opens with one of those classic western situations: a lone man heroically standing up for what is right and just against a mob that has taken the law into its own hands. Kirby Frye, the young, untested "boy sheriff" of Randado returns to town to find that in his absence a group of local citizens led by rancher Phil Sundeen has strung up two Mexicans awaiting trial on rustling charges in Frye's jail. Frye twice confronts Sundeen about the incident, but he is beaten and humiliated both times.

The moral issue raised by the lynching is overshadowed by the action adventures of the second half of the novel when Frye and a few men loyal to him set off after Sundeen and his men. One by one, the entire gang is tracked down and rounded up or killed. Everything leads up to the inevitable final confrontation between Frye and Sundeen. Here, however, Leonard pulls a switch: instead of trading bullets or fists, the two men engage in a whiskey-drinking contest. Sundeen loses, which enables Frye to serve him with a warrant for his arrest on the lynching charge.

The Law at Randado shows that Leonard still hadn't mastered the novel form. There are too many loose ends that aren't adequately developed, the plot moves fitfully, and the pacing of the action is erratic. Characterization is also still largely one-dimensional, with the good guys on one side and the bad guys on the other.

Escape from Five Shadows (1956) signals an important shift in Leonard's early fiction away from stock western situations; with its emphasis on characterization, it is a western in setting only. The main character, Corey Bowen, is a prisoner being held at the Five Shadows prison camp in the Arizona Territory. Innocent of the horse-stealing charge for which he was sentenced to an eight-year term, he is planning to become an ex-convict just as soon as he can figure out a way to escape.

Instead of focusing attention on the escape itself, Leonard concentrates on those characters who either want to prevent Bowen's escape, like Frank Renda, the brutal prison camp boss, or those who, for their own purposes, want to assist him. In the latter group are Earl Manring, convicted with Bowen on the horse-stealing charge, who plans to use his buddy to help him escape from Five Shadows; Karla Demery, the nineteen-year-old daughter of the nearby supply station owner who is romantically attracted to Bowen and who, convinced of his innocence, secretly tries to arrange a new trial for him; and Lizann Falvey, who offers to slip Bowen a gun if he will promise to kill her husband, the ineffectual government supervisor of the camp whom she has come to despise and from whom she longs to escape.

It is the complicated relationships between these characters and their secret dealings and double-dealings that interest Leonard more than the actual escape attempts. No mere good-guys-versus-bad-guys frontier drama, *Escape from Five Shadows* is a novel about characters looking for an edge in the game of survival, a theme Leonard would return to often in his later works.

Last Stand at Saber River (1959), on the other hand, *is* a good-guys-versus-bad-guys frontier drama and the most predictable and conventionally heroic of Leonard's western novels. It tells the story of Paul Cable who, with his wife and three young children in tow, returns to his Arizona home after serving with the Confederate Army in the Civil War. Upon his arrival, he finds that his property has been taken over by a gang of Yankee horse suppliers headed by the Kidston brothers, Vern and Duane. Despite the heavy odds against him, Cable vows to fight for his land and his family. Given plenty of opportunities for heroic action, he demonstrates his mettle and not unsurprisingly emerges victorious in the end.

The only really unpredictable elements in the novel are two of the secondary characters, Lorraine Kidston and Edward Janroe. Lorraine is Duane Kidston's bored and restless eighteen-year-old daughter. She sees in the struggle between Cable and her father and uncle an opportunity to spice up her life. Among other things, she tries to wedge herself between Cable and his wife. After being rebuffed in her efforts she drops from sight, though her type will again surface in some of Leonard's later novels.

More diabolical and more dangerous is Janroe. A veteran of the Confederate Army like Cable, he lost his left arm in battle; he also lost his command because of his sadistic tendencies (besides sending his men on suicide missions, he was also responsible for lining up and shooting 120 Union prisoners in his charge). The war is not over as far as he is concerned and he tries to use Cable in a plot to get rid of the Kidston brothers. When the extent of his villainy is ultimately disclosed, Cable and Vern Kidston put aside their differences and combine forces to destroy him.

Though the characters are neither subtly drawn nor very complicated and the plot is all too predictable, the novel is fast-paced and demonstrates Leonard's skill in handling action sequences. However, the whole affair is no more complicated than a routine half-hour episode from one of the many TV westerns that had come to dominate the home screen at the end of the 1950s.

Hombre (1961) is a much more compelling and original work. This final and most realistic of Leonard's 1950s westerns was written in 1959, though because of the decline in the western market, it took two years to find a publisher. (Ballantine finally purchased it for the bargain price of $1,250 and brought it out as a paperback original.) It also turned out to be the final work of fiction Leonard would publish for another five years.

The novel tells the story of John Russell, also known as "Hombre," a twenty-one-year-old white man raised by Apaches. He is one of six passengers riding on a stagecoach bound for Bisbee, Arizona, in 1884. Along the way the stage is attacked by a gang of highwaymen looking to grab the twelve thousand dollars in cash being carried by one of the passengers, Dr. Alexander Favor. Foiled in their attempt to get the money, the robbers kidnap Favor's wife, whom they then offer to trade for the cash. This sets up a tense situation as the two sides bargain for her life and for the money.

Hombre is a rarity among Leonard's fiction in that it is his only novel narrated in first person: the story is told by one of the passengers, a young man named Carl Allen. Seen only through Allen's eyes, Russell's character appears enigmatic for much of the novel. We are never quite sure how to judge this man of few words with his "tell-nothing-but-know-everything expression." In one scene in the novel (which Leonard said was the first scene he wrote and which he was prompted to write as a realistic corrective to the "white flag" situation he had seen hundreds of times on television), Frank Braden, the leader of the robbers, climbs up a hill and approaches Russell with a white flag of truce in his hand to negotiate for the money. When he turns to leave, Russell says, "I got a question. . . . How you going to get down that hill?"[6] Then he opens fires, wounding the fleeing Braden in the leg. The reader is left with the impression that Russell is a fellow who doesn't play by the rules, at least as far as they have been defined by television.

Russell is clearly no white-hatted Galahad out to right wrongs and rescue the defenseless. Early in the novel he refuses to become involved when Braden strongarms a stagecoach ticket from another passenger; "It wasn't my business,"[7] he explains. Later, the bandits tie Mrs. Favor up and leave her in the open sun without any water; they tell Russell that if he wants to save her life, he must bring out the twelve thousand dollars. He refuses. Though the other passengers criticize him for his heartlessness, no one else volunteers to take the money out. Finally, Russell makes a move to rescue the woman. He is killed in the process, but his heroic actions save the other passengers' lives.

Only then does Russell's character come into clear focus: what had all along appeared to be callous indifference was actually his cautious assessment of each situation. In the end, Carl Allen realizes that Russell was simply a man who "let people do or think what they wanted while he smoked a cigarette and thought it out calmly, without his feelings getting mixed up in it."[8] His final comment on Russell serves as a fitting epitaph: "He did what he felt had to be done. Even if it meant dying."[9]

Leonard normally avoids first-person narration because he doesn't want to be limited to a single point of view. His use of the technique in *Hombre,* however, is quite effective. Carl Allen remarks at the outset that he has been advised to imagine he is telling his story to a good friend; the result is a tale that is conversational in tone, informal and entirely convincing in its naturalness. Through his eyes Russell emerges as one of the most interesting and most realistically portrayed of all Leonard's western heroes: a man who does what has to be done. And does it on his terms.

Discouraged by his difficulty in getting *Hombre* published, Leonard decided it was time to try something different when he quit his job with Campbell-Ewald in 1961. However, instead of writing fiction as he planned, he found himself turning out educational films for Encyclopedia Brittanica and accepting free-lance advertising work to pay the bills. Fittingly, it was *Hombre* that rescued him from this situation: in 1965 Twentieth Century-Fox paid him ten thousand dollars for the film rights to the novel. The movie, directed by Martin Ritt and starring Paul Newman, was released the following year and became a popular hit. Ironically, this novel that experienced so much difficulty finding a publisher and that was largely responsible for Leonard's decision to move on to another fictional genre was selected in 1977 as one of the twenty-five best westerns of all time by the Western Writers of America.

Between "Trail of the Apache" and *Hombre,* Leonard produced an impressive body of work—over two dozen short stories and five novels. Along the way, his development as a writer was clearly in the direction of realism. While his prose had not yet reached the stripped-down level that would eventually characterize his style, it became increasingly leaner as the years went on. He soon stopped beginning his stories with the kind of elaborate scene setting he employed in "Trail of the Apache," which opens this way:

> Under the thatched roof ramada that ran the length of the agency office, Travisin slouched in a canvas-backed chair, his boots propped against one of the support posts. His gaze took in the sun-beaten, gray adobe buildings, all one-story structures, that rimmed the vacant quadrangle. It was a glaring, depressing scene of sun on rock, without a single shade tree or graceful feature to redeem the squat ugliness.[10]

Nor did he write many more ornate passages like this early example from "The Boy Who Smiled": "The sun glare was a white blistering shock that screamed its brightness."[11]

Hombre is a good example of Leonard's commitment to realism and his rejection of formula. No longer was he reluctant, as in his earlier stories, to show his protagonist in a bad light, as a man with flaws in his character. Nor was he hesitant about killing his hero off at the end, if the story demanded it. Though Leonard began the decade by learning how to work within the western genre, he ended it by displaying enough confidence in his writing to move beyond it. He was still developing as a writer, but he was doing so on his own terms without worrying about adhering to the narrow conventions of genre.

3

From Cowboys to Cops and Robbers

The period between 1966 and 1974—i.e. between *The Big Bounce,* Leonard's first crime novel, and *Fifty-Two Pickup,* his first major success in the genre, was one of varied opportunities and new successes. During these years he made the key transition from westerns to crime stories (though he would return to his old formula and write two more western novels). And he also began to enjoy his first successes as a Hollywood screenwriter.

In the mid-1960s, following the collapse of the western market, Leonard began writing a novel set in contemporary Michigan with the unusual title, *Mother, This Is Jack Ryan.* This was not, however, his first nonwestern work. In 1959 he published a story in *Short Stories Magazine* entitled "Bull Ring at Blisston," a contemporary tale set in rural Michigan about a migrant farm worker who was once a bullfighter. At the request of the owner of the farm where he works, he agrees to stage a bullfight for the owner's guests.

Though "Bull Ring at Blisston" was his sole nonwestern story published during the 1950s, Leonard wrote several others that he was unable to sell. In fact, the first story he wrote after graduating from college was a crime story set in Detroit. "Seven Letter Word for Corpse" is narrated in the first person by Stan Ellis, who returns to his hometown of Detroit to seek revenge against the man who shot and crippled his younger brother. The story is characterized by plenty of pulp-style tough talk and (almost nonexistent in his later work) the occasional colorful simile. (Ellis observes that an incriminating postmark on a letter stands out "like muscles on a shake dancer!") Though the story demonstrates that Leonard had a knack for such hard-boiled tales, he wasted little time in moving to westerns, where he felt there was a readier market for an unknown writer looking to make his first sale.

In 1954, following the publication of several western tales and his first western novel, Leonard again began working on short stories with a contemporary flavor. Though none could be described as crime stories, a few featured situations that, if developed differently, could have turned them into crime stories. In "Arma Virumque Cano," (the title comes from the opening line of Virgil's *Aeneid*), a Detroit businessman picks up a young female hitchhiker. When he stops to let her out, she tosses a pair of ripped panties into the back seat of his car and threatens to yell rape unless he hands over his wallet. In "For Something to Do," a young rural Michigan couple is terrorized by two men, one of whom is the wife's ex-boyfriend. Fortunately, the husband is able to roust the pair before anything serious happens.

Leonard also tried his hand at light comedy in "Evenings Away from Home," a whimsical story about a Detroit ad agency art director on location in Arizona who is victimized by a jealous boyfriend who mistakes him for someone else. "The Italian Cut" is about a minor domestic squabble between a young couple who argue about his bowling league and her new Italian-style haircut. Leonard dealt with a far more serious subject in "Time of Terror," a story about a planned political assassination set against the exotic background of Kuala Lampur.

In the mid-1960s, just before beginning *Mother, This Is Jack Ryan,* Leonard also wrote a couple of stories set in Spain. One, "The Only Good Syrian Footsoldier Is a Dead One," is a satirical look at the filming of a Roman epic being shot in Spain, the events seen through the eyes of a five-dollar-a-day extra from Royal Oak, Michigan. The other, "A Happy, Light-Hearted People," (whose title, Spanish setting, and seemingly aimless dialogue all echo Leonard's literary idol, Ernest Hemingway) is little more than a record of conversations between some British and American tourists in Spain about such topical subjects as the Beatles, the Profumo scandal in Britain, and Barry Goldwater's chances of being elected President.

In 1965 Leonard began *Mother, This Is Jack Ryan,* a novel about an ex-minor league baseball player, and ex-con, named Jack Ryan. Ryan hitches a ride north from Texas to his native Michigan with a crew of migrant workers and then joins them picking cucumbers on a farm near the small town of Geneva Beach, 150 miles north of the Detroit area where he grew up. Eventually he becomes involved with Nancy Hayes, the nineteen-year-old girlfriend of Ray Ritchie, owner of the farm where he works. A thrill-seeker looking for excitement, Nancy entices Ryan into a scheme to steal a fifty-thousand dollar cash payroll from Ritchie. Ryan, however, soon realizes he's become involved in a much more dangerous situation than he bargained for.

Jack Ryan is the first in a long line of ex-convicts to be featured as protagonists in Leonard's fiction. Ryan has a history of breaking and entering, nothing serious like armed robbery, though serious enough to land him in jail. In fact, when the novel opens, Ryan is in jail again, this time for attacking his crew leader with a baseball bat. Luckily for him, it is harvest season; the charges are dropped because none of the farm workers can be spared as witnesses for the police investigation into the incident.

Despite his criminal background, Ryan is basically a decent guy, though he is far removed from the hero in the white hat Leonard often employed in his western stories. Like many of Leonard's characters, Ryan is a passive type who simply drifts into situations: first, a couple of his fellow cucumber pickers talk him into breaking into a cottage where a beach party is taking place and stealing the wallets from the bedroom where the guests changed into their swimsuits; then he meets Nancy Hayes and is enticed into her plans for a big score.

Like several of the young women in Leonard's westerns (notably Lizann Falvey in *Escape from Five Shadows* and Lorraine Kidston in *Last Stand at Saber River*), Nancy Hayes is bored, restless, and looking for kicks. But she is also more self-absorbed, more cunning, more manipulative and far more dangerous than her predecessors. As a sixteen-year-old babysitter, she would come on to the fathers of the kids she watched, then inform the wives when their husbands took the bait and tried to make a pass at her. Just for fun. Later, bored with being Ray Ritchie's part-time mistress, she gets her kicks by tossing rocks through picture windows and by running a car off the road, seriously injuring one of the passengers. When she meets Jack Ryan, she decides a man with his breaking-and-entering experience might be useful in an exciting new plan.

At first, Ryan is tempted by her seductiveness. However, he gradually realizes how dangerous she is and concludes that the prospect of scoring fifty thousand dollars isn't worth the risks. His career as a minor league baseball player ended when he realized he couldn't hit the curve ball; now he decides he isn't going to make the mistake of falling for Nancy's shapely curves.

But Nancy has her own ideas. If Ryan won't play her game, she'll find another use for him: she invites him to her beach house one evening with the intention of killing him when he arrives. Shooting him, she concludes, "would be the biggest bounce of all." She casually guns down the first man who walks through the door (fortunately it isn't Ryan), her only emotion curiosity as to whether his eyes will be open or closed. Jack Ryan is lucky to have survived his encounter with Nancy Hayes, though he will have to face another dangerous situation eight years later when he makes a return appearance in *Unknown Man No. 89*.

Despite his high hopes for the novel, Leonard's agent H. N. Swanson was unable to interest any publisher or film producer in the manuscript. In a matter of a few short months, it was rejected eighty-four times. "The unanimous negative reaction of eighty-four professionals," Leonard remarked, "would suggest that I hide the manuscript away, maybe even *throw* it away, and move on to something with a more commercial ring to it."[1] Instead, he set to work revising the manuscript, though he resisted the suggestion made by some editors that he turn Ryan into more of a hero.

In a letter to Swanson in January 1967, Leonard spelled out

detailed plans for revision. First of all, he changed the title from the cumbersome *Mother, This Is Jack Ryan* to *The Big Bounce.* The idea for the new title came from an article he read in the February 1967 issue of *Esquire* entitled "The New American Woman." Included in the essay was a description of the new LA Woman who, when boredom threatens, will "seek the kick, the bounce, the flash." Nancy Hayes's search for the "big bounce" now became the focus of the revised work. He also strengthened the story line, developed the characters better, and related them more closely to the action. His revisions resulted in an exciting contemporary thriller that in August 1967 Swanson was able to sell, first to Warner Brothers (for fifty thousand dollars) and then to Fawcett Books, which brought it out as a Gold Medal paperback in 1969.

Instead of following up *The Big Bounce* with a second contemporary novel, Leonard wrote another western. "At that time," he confesses, "ideas didn't come to me the way they do now. I didn't see situations as I do now all the time. I wasn't yet used to thinking in today terms."[2] So, like Raymond Chandler who "cannibalized" his early short stories for his novels, Leonard began looking through his western tales for ideas. He found one story, "Only Good Ones," originally published in a 1961 collection entitled *Western Roundup,* which he felt he could expand into a novel.

Actually, "Only Good Ones" was a prequel to a 1954 *Argosy* story of his, "Saint with a Six-Gun," a tale about the hanging of a character named Bobby Valdez. In "Only Good Ones," Leonard set the action three years before the hanging. Obviously intrigued with the character of Valdez, Leonard now decided to resurrect him again, make him older, and expand the incident described in "Only Good Ones" into a novel he would call *Valdez Is Coming.*

Valdez Is Coming, published as a Fawcett paperback in 1970, is the most conventionally heroic of Leonard's westerns. Bob Valdez is part-time constable in a small Arizona town. Due to a misunderstanding, he guns down a black man who has been mistakenly identified as a murderer. When he discovers that the man is survived by a pregnant Indian wife, he takes it upon himself to try to raise five hundred dollars for the woman. He decides the main contributor ought to be Frank Tanner, who fingered the innocent man as a killer in the first place. Tanner, however, twice rebuffs Valdez's appeals, the second time sending him off torturously strapped to a makeshift cross. Now more determined than ever, Valdez sends Tanner the message, "Valdez is coming." And come he does. He guns down a dozen of Tanner's men before confronting him one last time with his request for a contribution.

Creating a heroic protagonist was certainly nothing new for Leonard; about all that differentiates Valdez from his predecessors are far greater odds to overcome (there are two dozen men on his trail) and a much larger number of bad guys he has to kill (a dozen). The novel also reworks scenes from Leonard's previous novels. For example, the humiliating treatment Valdez receives when he approaches Tanner with his appeal for a contribution duplicates the way Kirby Frye was treated by Phil Sundeen in *The Law at Randado.* Also, Valdez's plan of kidnapping Tanner's woman and using her as a bargaining chip to force him to cough up the money previously figured in *Hombre.* Though *Valdez Is Coming* was another of Leonard's western works to be made into a successful film (this one with Burt Lancaster in the title role), the novel suggests that Leonard might have been tiring of the western genre.

A Hollywood producer, beat out by another in his attempt to purchase movie rights to *Valdez Is Coming,* asked Leonard for something like *Valdez,* only different. At the Birmingham Library one night, Leonard came across a book by Harry M. Caudill entitled *Night Comes to the Cumberlands,* which contained a chapter on the great Moonshine Wars during Prohibition. That's it, Leonard thought, and promptly sat down and wrote a nine-and-a-half page outline for a novel. MGM liked the outline and bought screen rights even before Leonard wrote the novel, which he would title *The Moonshine War.* It eventually appeared as a Fawcett paperback in 1969.

In *The Moonshine War,* Leonard returned once again to the past, this time to Kentucky in the early 1930s rather than the Arizona of the 1880s he ordinarily used in his westerns. Thanks to Prohibition, the moonshine industry in the Kentucky hills is booming. For Son Martin, things look especially good: he is sitting on a hidden cache of 150 barrels of eight-year-old whiskey produced by his late father. His problem is that the whiskey, with a market value in excess of $120,000, has attracted a trio of interested parties who intend to steal it.

Though not a western, *The Moonshine War* shares several features in common with Leonard's western works. Like many of his cowboy predecessors, Son Martin is a stand-up guy who isn't going to be bullied, no matter how great the odds against him. His opponents are a gang of ex-convicts led by a trio of tough guys: Frank Long, a former Army buddy of Martin's, now a Federal Prohibition agent whose interest in Martin's whiskey is purely personal; Dr. Emmett Taulbee, an ex-dentist who is now a big-time whiskey runner; and Dual Meaders, who'd just as soon shoot you as say "good morning" to you. Like Popeye, the sociopathic bootlegger in William Faulkner's *Sanctuary,* Meaders does whatever his fancy urges him to. For instance, he once spent time in prison for pouring gasoline on a sleeping hobo and setting him afire simply because he didn't like hoboes.

Despite the odds against him, Son Martin vows that the hijackers won't get his whiskey without a fight. While the local residents look on with a mixture of curiosity and self-interest (the hijackers have been trying to force Martin to disclose the location of the hidden whiskey by systematically destroying his neighbors' stills), Martin, assisted only by his black hired man Aaron, digs in for battle. The explosive finale to the novel is worthy of any gun-blazing western epic.

Neither a character study, though many of the characters are interesting figures, nor a simple period drama, *The Moonshine War* is, like Leonard's westerns, an action-packed adventure story that builds to an exciting finale. Leonard also takes full advantage of the backwoods setting to create several colorful local characters and to fill the novel with some good-old-boy antics, as well as plenty of down-home humor, especially in the dialogue.

The Moonshine War also provided Leonard with his break into films as a screenwriter: for the first time he was hired to write a screenplay based on one of his own works. The film, a 1970 MGM release directed by Richard Quine and starring Alan Alda, Richard Widmark, and Patrick McGoohan, remained generally faithful to the novel, though the authenticity of the piece was severely compromised by the phony Kentucky accents employed by the actors.

Forty Lashes Less One, Leonard's next novel, was written in 1968, immediately after *The Moonshine War,* but it wasn't published by Bantam until 1972. Though marketed as a western, except for its Arizona setting it has little in common with Leonard's previous western works. The year is 1909, several decades later than the usual period of his westerns, and the action takes place not in the colorful canyons and mesas of Arizona but almost entirely inside the Yuma territorial prison.

Unlike most of Leonard's westerns, *Forty Lashes Less One* contains no heroes. And with the exception of Everett Manly, a do-good Pentecostal preacher and ex-missionary who is apppointed superintendent of the Yuma prison (simply because he lived in the area and was willing to take the job on a temporary basis), it also contains no good guys. What it does have in abundance is an assortment of outlaws and outcasts. The treat for the reader comes in watching what happens when Leonard brings these characters together.

Chief among the outlaws is Frank Shelby, who is serving a forty-five-year sentence for armed robbery and murder. A shrewd con man who virtually runs the prison's affairs himself, he intends to make a break for freedom when the prisoners are being transferred to the new penitentiary at Florence. He obtains the inside information he needs from Norma Davis, an ex-prostitute serving a sentence for armed robbery and attempted murder. He gets her to trade sexual favors for information from the prison turnkey.

The outcasts include Harold Jackson, a black man, and Raymond

San Carlos, an Indian. Both are victims of racism: Jackson deserted the US Army after not being allowed off a troop ship while it was docked at Tampa, Florida for ten days simply because he was black; San Carlos has been made to feel so ashamed of his Apache heritage that he hides the fact that his father was once a member of Geronimo's band. The two men are pitted against each other by Shelby and start out as hated enemies. Gradually, however, they come to recognize their common plight and become allies. After Shelby's escape, they volunteer to go after him, though they do so only for their own reasons. In the end, they return him, then turn and ride off to freedom together.

In some ways, *Forty Lashes Less One* is as important a transitional novel in Leonard's writing as *The Big Bounce* was. For one thing, the novel reveals Leonard's growing interest in the types of nonheroic characters he would come to focus on more and more. Also, without a hero to worry about, he is freer to adopt a less-reverent tone in his writing. Even though the setting of the novel is a tough prison, Leonard treats situations with a kind of grim humor. He never stoops to the silly antics of, say, the sitcom *Hogan's Heroes,* where the simpleminded humor trivialized its prison setting. Leonard's humor arises from his characters and their interaction. And from their dialogue. These men and women are tough, worldly types who aren't afraid to speak their minds; if what they say is offensive, it's also convincingly realistic.

Because it was such a departure from his previous work in the genre, Leonard's western fans may not have found *Forty Lashes Less One* entirely to their liking. But for those who enjoyed the new approach he began to take in *The Big Bounce,* the novel represented another step in Leonard's development into one of the most original of crime writers.

Though he was still anything but a household name as a novelist, Leonard in the early 1970s began making a name for himself as a screenwriter. Quickly on the heels of his debut success with the screenplay for *The Moonshine War,* he sold several more, though most never made it to the screen. In 1970, for example, he wrote two original screenplays: *The Sun-King Man* and *Jesus Saves,* the latter about a television evangelist who uses a born-again rock musician with a reputation for preaching and faith healing to pump new life into his sagging ministry.

The following year, he turned out two more original scripts: *Picket Line,* about a farm workers' strike at a Texas melon ranch led by a Cesar Chavez–type character named Vincent Mora (the same name he would later use for the main character in *Glitz*); and *American Flag* (sold to Steve McQueen for forty thousand dollars), a western about a man who takes on the entire American Flag Mining Company in a dispute over his mining claim. Leonard also earned hefty sums by selling the film rights to the two westerns he wrote during this period: *Valdez Is Coming,* released as a film in 1971, and *Forty Lashes Less One,* which was never produced.

Joe Kidd was the first of Leonard's original screenplays to make it to the screen; directed by John Sturges and starring Clint Eastwood in the title role, it was released in 1972. A perfect vehicle for the tough, laconic film-hero image Eastwood was developing, the film further enhanced Leonard's reputation as a promising screenwriter.

Joe Kidd hires on with Frank Harlan and his men who are trying to halt the activities of Luis Chama, leader of a group of local Mexican settlers fighting to keep their land against the onslaught of the white invaders. Kidd decides to join up with Harlan because Chama once stole some of his horses, but as soon as he begins to witness Harlan's violent tactics, he realizes he signed on with the wrong side. But before he can do anything about it, he is disarmed and taken prisoner by Harlan, who decides to kill five innocent Mexican villagers three times a day until Chama surrenders to him. Despite the odds, in true Clint Eastwood fashion Joe Kidd stops Harlan and heroically saves the day.

Eastwood liked Leonard's script and asked for another. Leonard responded with a screenplay about a melon farmer who gets tangled up with a hit man for the mob. When Eastwood later decided to pass on the project, Leonard sold the screenplay, entitled *Mr. Majes-*

tyk, to producer Walter Mirisch; the film was released in 1974 with Charles Bronson in the title role.

In a reversal of his usual practice, Leonard then turned his screenplay into a novel. Vincent Majestyk (not to be confused with the Walter Majestyk who gives Jack Ryan a job at his small motel in *The Big Bounce*) is a small-time farmer who simply wants to get his 160 acres of melons picked before they rot. But as is the case with many of Leonard's characters, circumstances conspire against him. First, he is arrested for assaulting a man who tried to force him to hire a crew of pickers he didn't want. Then, on the way to his court hearing, the bus the prisoners are being transported on is hijacked by friends of one of the passengers, Frank Renda, a mob hit man. (Though they share the same name, this Frank Renda is not the same Frank Renda who was the brutal prison boss in *Escape from Five Shadows.*)

Majestyk and Renda end up taking off with the bus. Later, however, Majestyk decides to do the right thing and return his companion to the police. Before he can do this, Renda escapes and vows to get even with Majestyk for trying to turn him in. Majestyk thus finds himself presented (as were Son Martin and Joe Kidd before him) with his own opportunity to prove he has what it takes to overcome the odds against him. In standard Hollywood fashion, he of course succeeds.

Leonard's novelization, published as a Dell paperback in 1974, stuck closely to the screenplay, though the locale was changed from Colorado to the more familiar Arizona and some key changes were made in the character of Renda. In the film, Renda is pure viciousness, a cold-blooded killer whose obsession with Majestyk borders on the maniacal. In the novel, Leonard tones down Renda's character in order to humanize him some, a practice he would continue to follow in the portrayal of most of his future villains.

Despite his increased activity as a screenwriter in the early 1970s, Leonard resisted the temptation to move to Hollywood, choosing instead to remain in Birmingham, Michigan. He would often fly to Hollywood in the morning for a studio meeting, then catch a plane and return home later the same day. Hollywood was good to him, financially speaking, but he insisted on maintaining his detachment. He didn't want to become too involved in the business of filmmaking. "That's all they talk about out there," he says. "I should be on my own, working on my stories."[3]

Leonard's film work was his primary source of income during these years, though he always kept in mind Raymond Chandler's admonition: when you go to Hollywood, wear your second-best suit, artistically speaking. He also learned that you should never allow anyone to pick you up at the airport, especially in a gray stretch limo: "Limos are seductive," he warned, "they make you feel important, and the next thing you know you're taking yourself too seriously."[4] The only thing he wanted to take seriously was the fiction that, thanks to the financial support he received from his film work, he was able to continue writing.

4

Crime Begins to Pay

After more than two decades at his craft, Leonard had mastered several important lessons about writing: from Hemingway he learned the value of using dialogue and simple, unadorned language to tell a story; from the movies he learned that a story constructed as a sequence of scenes moves at a rapid pace. Then in 1972, at his agent's suggestion, he read a novel that taught him another lesson that would help make his writing even more effective.

George V. Higgins's *The Friends of Eddie Coyle,* a comic novel about a small-time Boston hoodlum, is presented largely through dialogue and extended monologues. Using plenty of dialogue was nothing new to Leonard, but Higgins demonstrated how effective graphically realistic (and frequently obscene) dialogue could be. Higgins's characters' subjective monologues also reminded Leonard that describing events from a character's point of view rather than his own could enhance the realism of the work.

In an early scene in his new novel, *Fifty-Two Pickup,* Leonard had to describe a character walking across Woodward Avenue in Detroit. At first he worried about getting all the details of the description accurate so readers familiar with the location wouldn't be disappointed. It then occurred to him that if he described the scene from his *character*'s point of view rather than his own, the reader would not only see the scene, he would learn something about the character through whose eyes the scene was being presented. By thus withdrawing from the page, he could turn more of the actual story telling over to his characters.

Fifty-Two Pickup (1974) is a hard-edged thriller about the efforts of a businessman to extricate himself from a nasty situation. Harry Mitchell owns a small auto parts manufacturing company just outside Detroit. For the first time in his twenty-two-year marriage to his wife Barbara, he has become involved with another woman, a young nude model named Cini Fisher. The novel opens with Mitchell arriving at Cini's apartment with the intention of ending their affair. Cini, however, isn't home; instead he is greeted by a trio of masked men who show him a home movie documenting his involvement with her. Unless he pays them $105,000, they'll send the film to his wife.

Up to this point, there isn't anything particularly original about the blackmail situation. But then Leonard introduces some unexpected twists. Harry Mitchell turns out to be the wrong guy to lean on; he deflates the blackmail scam by confessing his affair to his wife and refusing to pay the blackmailers a cent. His antagonists, however, prove to be equally capable of doing the unexpected: first, they steal his gun and then, in a brutally chilling scene, force him to watch a film of Cini being shot several times in cold blood with the gun. Now if he refuses to pay what they demand, they'll send evidence to the police that will put him in jail for Cini's murder.

Harry Mitchell is the type of character who should be familiar to readers of Leonard's westerns: a decent, mild-mannered guy until someone steps over the line and challenges him. Then he becomes a take-charge, stand-up individual who isn't going to let anyone ruin his life or the business he has worked so hard to build up. An ex–fighter pilot and a veteran of eleven years on an automotive assembly line, Harry has a tough, no-nonsense attitude:

> I don't expect any gifts or favors. Nothing is free. But I also don't expect any shit from anybody. No, I take that back. I *do* expect it. What I mean is, when it comes it doesn't come as a surprise. I watch where I'm walking and I don't step in it if I can help it. Why should anybody take any shit if they can help it?[1]

Harry's no angel. We aren't asked to overlook his affair with Cini; he made a mistake and he regrets it. One can, however, sympathize with someone forced to pay such a high price for his mistake, and pull for him in his efforts to outsmart his opponents.

If *Fifty-Two Pickup* were a typical mystery story, Harry would likely seek the help of a private detective to get the blackmailers off his back. However, he's a man who does things his own way without anyone else's help. His wife's description of his tennis playing can be applied to the way he handles problems: "He was an unorthodox player who slapped at the ball instead of stroking it, but God he hit it hard and he was all over the court."[2]

Harry begins by snooping around to learn the names of his blackmailers. Then, using wits and savvy, the same qualities he employed to solve a potentially explosive union problem at his plant, he deals with his personal difficulties. But unlike Leonard's western heroes, Harry never has to fire a gun. Instead, he opens his books to the leader of the blackmailers and convinces him that all he can raise is fifty-two thousand dollars in cash; then he talks separately to the other two blackmailers, sowing seeds of distrust among all three. His actions demonstrate, as a character in one of Leonard's later novels puts it, that "wonderful things happen when you plant seeds of distrust in a garden of assholes."[3]

Leonard had created a number of villains before *Fifty-Two Pickup,* but none quite like the trio of Alan Raimy, Bobby Shy, and Leo Frank: Raimy, a former accountant with an MA in Business Administration, is the brains; Shy the muscle; Frank, who operates a nude modeling studio, supplies the bait in the person of one of his employees, Cini Fisher. These guys might at first appear to be a ragtag bunch of amateurs, but like Harry Mitchell, there's more to them than meets the eye.

Though Leo Frank turns out to be exactly what Raimy calls him, "a fat-ass juice head who was liable to melt with a little heat,"[4] Raimy and Shy prove to be vicious men who will do whatever it takes to salvage their blackmail scheme. Bobby Shy nearly smothers his girlfriend to death with a pillow in order to force information from her, then later cold-bloodedly guns Leo down when he starts to get too skittish. Raimy poses a different threat. To get even with

Mitchell for trying to con him, he kidnaps his wife, pumps her full of heroin, and then abuses her sexually. Harry may be tough, but these aren't lightweights he's up against. It'll take more than a tough attitude to defeat his antagonists and rescue his wife.

Leonard displays a surer novelistic hand in *Fifty-Two Pickup* than he did in his earlier efforts in the crime genre. Character, setting, and dialogue all have an air of convincing authenticity. Individual scenes can be singled out for special praise (*Newsweek*'s Peter Prescott doesn't overstate matters when he claims that the scene where Harry is forced to watch the film of Cini's murder "may be the most alarming in any American crime novel"),[5] but each fits neatly into the well-constructed plot. Neither character nor incident is wasted as Leonard deftly weaves Harry's personal and professional crises into a compelling story.

Though the film rights to the novel were originally sold in 1973, it wasn't until 1986 that *Fifty-Two Pickup* finally made it to the big screen. The movie, which starred Roy Scheider and Ann-Margret and was directed by John Frankenheimer, is one of the most successful cinematic treatments of any of Leonard's work. Though credited with being coauthor of the screenplay, Leonard actually wrote only a few scenes and touched up some of the dialogue. Nevertheless, despite some minor changes (the setting, for example, is switched from Michigan to California), the film remained faithful to the novel. It retained much of its dialogue and effectively captured the hard-hitting realism of Leonard's first important success in the crime genre.

Leonard's next novel, *Swag* (1976; retitled *Ryan's Rules* when it was reprinted in a Dell paperback edition in 1978), is an offbeat version of the American Dream. Two guys—Frank J. Ryan and Ernest Stickley, Jr., known as "Stick"—meet by chance: Ryan interrupts Stick as he's stealing a car from the used-car lot where Ryan works as a salesman. Ryan admires Stick's nerve, and thinks he just might have found the partner he's been looking for. As he explains to Stick, two guys who are "frank with each other and earnest about their work"[6] can expect to earn three to five grand a week.

(Leonard's original title for the novel was *The Frank and Earnest Method.*) Stick, down to his last eight dollars, likes Ryan's proposition and agrees to join him in his new business venture—armed robbery.

Frank Ryan (not to be confused with Jack Ryan of *The Big Bounce* and, later, *Unknown Man No. 89,* though one of Jack Ryan's former criminal partners, Leon Woody, does figure prominently in *Swag*) has even done some market research before choosing his new career. He tells Stick that there were over twenty-three thousand reported robberies in Detroit the previous year and argues that statistics prove that for the amount of risk involved, armed robbery pays the highest dividends. If he and Stick follow his Ten Rules for Success and Happiness (ranging from "Always Be Polite" to "Never Associate with People Known to Be in Crime"), their new enterprise can't fail.

Though he lacks Ryan's long-range vision, Stick, who has served time in prison for auto theft, brings experience to the partnership. He'd really just like to get to Pompano Beach, Florida, to see his seven-year-old daughter (that was the reason he was stealing the car from Ryan in the first place), but decides he can't pass up the promising opportunity Ryan offers him.

Their initial effort, a liquor-store robbery, nets them over six thousand dollars. "If they're all this easy," Frank tells Stick, "I believe we found our calling."[7] Despite their inexperience, these guys aren't incompetents like the bumbling Dortmunder gang whose comic antics are chronicled in Donald Westlake's hilarious caper novels. Stick and Ryan are cool, capable of adjusting whenever anything goes wrong. For example, to pull off the robbery of a supermarket, Ryan is momentarily pressed into duty as a cashier; slipping immediately into the role of conscientious employee, he begins arguing with a customer about an expired coupon. On another occasion, the pair avert a potential setback when a competitor beats them to the punch and robs the bar they intended to rob: they sit back, wait for him to finish, then rob him.

As their successes multiply, Stick and Ryan begin enjoying the fruits of their endeavors: they select flashy new wardrobes, purchase an expensive new Thunderbird, and move into an apartment in a swinging-singles complex. Here they spend their leisure time (which is considerable, given their line of work) lounging around the pool and partying with the nurses, cocktail waitresses, and dental hygienists who inhabit the place. Stick and Ryan have indeed attained the "good life" promised to those with enough initiative to go after the American Dream.

Their troubles begin when they seek to expand their operation. After an impressive string of thirty-one successful robberies of liquor stores, supermarkets, party stores and the like, Ryan feels it's time to move up to something bigger: he has in mind the J. L. Hudson Department Store in downtown Detroit. Though he has his doubts, Stick, as usual, decides to go along with the plan.

But once they take on new partners—two black men, Sportree, an old friend of Ryan's, and Leon Woody, who once worked with Jack Ryan, plus a Puerto Rican ex-boxer named Carmen Billy Ruiz—things begin to go wrong. During the holdup at Hudson's, two people are killed, including Ruiz, who is shot in the back by Woody. Then when Stick returns to Hudson's two days later to retrieve the cash that was supposed to have been hidden away, the police are waiting for him.

Stick concludes that he and Ryan have been duped out of the stolen loot by Woody and Sportree. ("Don't ever do business with a colored guy," Stick observes, "especially one who's smarter than you are.")[8] Worse, he realizes his new partners will now have to kill him to keep him from telling the police what he knows about them. The party's over. Stick now has to figure out a way to save his neck, which sets up the explosive conclusion to the novel.

Though on the face of it a crime novel (it includes almost three dozen armed robberies and six murders), *Swag* is also a novel of character and manners. Because it devotes so much time to the description of the private lives of Leonard's two fun-loving bachelors who have suddenly struck it rich, the novel lacks the narrative intensity of *Fifty-Two Pickup*. However, what *Swag* loses in dramatic tension and suspense it more than makes up for in its increased attention to character and the small details of everyday life.

Leonard's humorous portrayal of the relationship between Stick and Ryan, who end up bickering like newlyweds over such domestic matters as which one is spending the most money and who gets to drive the car, has the effect of giving the novel a solid realistic foundation. His depiction of the pool-and-party scene at Stick's and Ryan's apartment complex also adds a touch of satire to the novel.

Stick and Ryan certainly aren't heroes. But because Leonard makes them so convincing as human beings and because he describes everything from their perspective, the reader views them sympathetically. When a pair of thugs try to rob Stick in a shopping-center parking lot, we are as upset as he is at becoming a victim of street crime; like him, we conveniently overlook the fact that he himself has just stolen the money from somebody else. One is also apt to find oneself nodding in agreement with the backwards logic of Ryan's reply to Stick's complaint that he doesn't get to drive the car as often as his partner: "You want a car," Frank tells him, "steal one. You want it bad enough, *buy* one, for Christ sake."[9]

The main advancement in *Swag* over Leonard's earlier work comes in his portrayal of his criminal characters as convincing human beings. Comic elements—especially in the dialogue—are also given greater play. The specific influence of George V. Higgins can be detected in Leonard's decision to allow his characters to talk more (though he never gives them the meandering monologues that are a characteristic of Higgins's work). Also, the lines he gives his characters to speak are notably more obscene than previously, which also adds to their believability.

Like *Fifty-Two Pickup, Swag* began to earn Leonard some important critical attention. *Publishers Weekly* praised it as a "streetwise, electrifying novel"[10] and Newgate Callendar of the *New York Times,* an early admirer of Leonard, said the novel "will have the critics mentioning Chandler and Higgins—it's that good."[11] Leonard was slowly earning a reputation as a crime writer worth watching.

Leonard had sold the film rights to *Fifty-Two Pickup* in 1974 to Noah Films, an Israeli production company. The producers decided to move the setting from Detroit to Tel Aviv and to change the main character from an auto parts manufacturer to the US Ambassador to Israel. Leonard spent three weeks in Israel working on the project, which was subsequently shelved. (The Israeli material eventually resulted in a film titled *The Ambassador,* starring Robert Mitchum and Rock Hudson, which was released in 1984. By that time it bore absolutely no resemblance to *Fifty-Two Pickup*.) Leonard's trip to Israel wasn't wasted, however: "I liked the atmosphere," he said, "guys walking along the beach with machine guns. I could see where I could introduce some new characters for me."[12] He returned to Israel and spent several weeks researching material for a new novel, *The Hunted,* which came out as a Dell paperback in 1977.

"The hunted" referred to in the title is a mortgage broker named Al Rosen who has been hiding out in Israel for three years, ever since he testified against two crime figures before a federal grand jury in Detroit. Unfortunately for Rosen, his whereabouts are discovered by one of the men he testified against. The man travels to Israel with two hit men to kill Rosen. However, their job is made more difficult when a marine guard at the US Embassy named David E. Davis, a restless Vietnam veteran looking for combat excitement, befriends Rosen and decides to help him.

The action of the novel develops slowly and the plot lacks the clever twists of *Fifty-Two Pickup*. The characters also never come to life the way those in *Fifty-Two Pickup* and *Swag* do. (Leonard also concedes he made a mistake in not allowing Rosen to remain the main character instead of switching the focus to Davis, a too-obvious hero type.) And though the setting is fresh, the situations are strongly reminiscent of his westerns, where the good guys routinely squared off against the bad guys under the hot desert sun. There are some good lines of dialogue, most of them given to Kamal Rashad, a black hit man from Detroit, but the novel lacks the conversational punch of Leonard's previous two books. All in all, *The Hunted* is a relatively uninspired effort.

Leonard isn't ordinarily inclined to use autobiographical elements in his fiction. However, his next novel, *Unknown Man No. 89* (1977), another crime story set in Detroit, is a notable exception. For the first time in his career, he gives his protagonist personal experiences closely modeled on his own, which adds an emotional dimension not found in any of his previous works.

Jack Ryan, who previously appeared in *The Big Bounce,* returns as the main character in *Unknown Man No. 89*. It is several years after the events depicted in the earlier novel and Ryan has given up his brief career of breaking and entering. He's now a process server in Detroit. He enjoys his work and as long as he follows his number one rule, "Never get personally involved," things go smoothly. ("Don't get too close and start feeling sorry for people," he cautions himself. "You want to do that, go work for the Salvation Army.")[13]

One day, a very profitable opportunity comes Ryan's way. A Louisiana "investment counselor" named Francis X. Perez arrives in Detroit looking for a missing man named Bobby Leary: Perez has information about valuable unclaimed stock Leary owns and offers Ryan fifteen thousand dollars to find him. Ryan jumps at the opportunity, though he has second thoughts once he begins to hear reports about several vicious murders Leary has apparently been responsible for.

But Ryan doesn't have to worry about Leary for long: Leary turns up dead in the morgue, a murder victim (the tag on his toe designating him "Unknown man No. 89" gives the novel its title). Ryan's troubles, however, are far from over. Leary was killed by Virgil Royal, his former partner, who thinks Leary cheated him out of his share of the loot they grabbed in a bank robbery. Now he intends to get what is owed him from the money he believes Ryan wanted to pay Leary.

Things are further complicated by the presence of Leary's widow Denise, a pretty young alcoholic who is now legally entitled to the $150,000 owed her husband. Perez would like to get the drunken woman's signature on a document giving him power of attorney.

With it he can keep all the money himself. Ryan, despite his rule against such things, has become emotionally involved with Denise Leary. He decides to turn the tables on Perez and cheat *him* out of the whole sum. Thus emerges another of those typical Leonard situations where several competing parties angle to get their hands on the jackpot.

Unknown Man No. 89 contains its share of violent characters (in addition to Bobby Leary, whose murderous deeds are only recounted, there is Virgil Royal and Perez's sidekick Raymond Gidre, cold-blooded killers both) and gripping action. What gives the novel a new twist that sets it apart from its predecessors is the intimate glimpse it offers into the experience of its two alcoholics, Ryan and Denise Leary.

Ryan, off booze for over three years, is well on his way to winning his battle with the bottle. Denise, however, is in bad shape: she spends her days and nights drinking in cheap Cass Corridor bars. There is a stark contrast between her behavior when drunk and when she begins to sober up, which with Ryan's help she manages to do. Ryan is no white knight in shining armor who can rescue her from the menacing dragons; but as one who has battled his own demons, he can offer support in her private struggle against hers.

Unknown Man No. 89 was written at the time Leonard fought and won his own battle with alcohol. In fact, he says that some of the scenes of Ryan and Denise at AA meetings are based virtually word for word on his own experiences. This distinctly personal element adds considerable emotional impact to the novel. It isn't Leonard's style to preach. However, he gets his message about the effects of alcohol abuse across by his vivid depiction of the self-destructive behavior of an alcoholic like Denise.

Unknown Man No.89 has the distinction of being one of the final film projects Alfred Hitchcock worked on before his death. It isn't clear exactly what interested Hitchcock about the novel, which has little in common with his usual work. What he apparently liked, as reported by Donald Spoto in his biography of the famed director, was the character of Denise Leary, and especially the scene where the drunken woman fends off Ryan with an obscene joke. Hitchcock died before the project ever developed beyond its initial stage, and the novel was never filmed.

On the surface at least, Leonard's next novel, *The Switch* (1978) is, like *Fifty-Two Pickup,* a story about a crime caper that goes haywire. Mickey Dawson, attractive wife of a successful Bloomfield Hills, Michigan, building contractor, is kidnapped by the usual motley trio of Leonard bad guys: two ex-cons (one black, one white) and a psychopathic Nazi cultist. However, unbeknownst to them (or even to Mickey herself), husband Frank filed for divorce just before flying to the Bahamas for a week-long tryst with his new girlfriend. Instead of being upset by the kidnappers' threat to kill Mickey unless he pays them one million dollars, Frank figures they are doing him a big favor.

However, whenever a caper goes awry in a Leonard novel, there usually follows a twist that makes things even more interesting. Here it is provided by Frank's girlfriend Melanie, who convinces one of the kidnappers that Frank will probably cough up at least $100,000 if they'll kill Mickey: this would save Frank a fortune in alimony payments, plus smooth the way if she should decide to marry him. However, this plan also goes haywire when Mickey escapes, only throwing things into further confusion.

As usual, Leonard keeps things moving with plenty of unexpected plot developments as the various parties try to keep their schemes afloat. But in contrast to *Fifty-Two Pickup,* where the action was presented largely from Harry Mitchell's point of view, in *The Switch* the reader sees things both from the kidnappers' perspective as they try to salvage their plan and from the kidnap victim's point of view. Also, in *The Switch* the kidnapped wife isn't used primarily as an excuse for the husband's heroics in extricating the two of them from a tight spot, as she was in *Fifty-Two Pickup*. Far more than just a convenient victim demanded by the plot, Mickey Dawson becomes the primary focus of the novel.

Prior to her ordeal, Mickey was the perfect country-club wife to her husband Frank and a devoted tennis-mom to their thirteen-year-old son Bo. Though she never feels at ease among the small-talk set at the club, she goes through the motions because she knows that's what is expected of her. She has suppressed her own identity for so long that she is in danger of completely losing all sense of self. Even though she resents her Big-Dealer husband and is tired of their empty relationship, she cannot bring herself to rock the boat by confronting him directly. Unable to express her feelings openly, she resigns herself to continue playing "kissy-ass."

Once she is kidnapped, however, things change. Her imprisonment ironically becomes a liberating experience, freeing her from a confining self-image. It takes a kidnapping to transform "nice" Mickey into "the Mickey she always wanted to be." When her feelings about her husband finally force from her the uncharacteristic remark, "He's an asshole," she is both surprised and relieved. "She continued to hear the word she had said out loud for the first time in her life and began wondering if she could improve on it."[14] Watching her develop into an independent woman is one of the genuine pleasures of the book.

Kathy Warbelow, reviewing *The Switch* for the *Detroit Free Press,* Leonard's hometown newspaper, faulted him for the novel's sexual attitudes, which she described as being "about as liberated as Mickey Spillane's" and for defining his female characters "mostly in terms of their physical attributes."[15] This criticism certainly has some validity, especially in the case of Melanie, who is routinely described as a "foxy chick" with "great big ones."

Leonard concedes that Warbelow's criticism has since caused him to pay closer attention to his portrayal of female characters. However, her comments should not detract from his largely successful attempt to portray Mickey's self-discovery with sympathy and insight. Mickey's decision to join the kidnappers at the end in a scheme to snatch Frank's girlfriend isn't entirely credible. What *is* very credible, however, is her switch from a cipher to a real woman by the end of the novel.

The Switch demonstrates that Leonard was neither trapped by a formula nor confined by the limitations of the crime genre. While the crime elements of the novel are up to his usual high standards (the novel was nominated for an Edgar Allan Poe Award by the Mystery Writers of America as the best paperback mystery of the year), *The Switch* offers something more. In addition to its skilled portrayal of a woman's self-discovery, it also displays Leonard's skills at social satire.

Leonard first revealed a talent for social satire in *Swag*, where he aimed his barbs at the swinging-singles scene. Here his target is the upper-middle-class country-club set, where conversations (at least those reported in *The Switch*) seldom rise above the mundane. Writing about the seamy side of life, Leonard admits, is far more interesting than trying to describe country-club life. Leonard confessed to having a difficult time writing the dialogue for scenes set at the club. "What do the people talk about?" he wondered. He found a solution to his problem by presenting the action from Mickey's point of view, which allows her impatience with the idle and inane conversations to color the scene. This achieves Leonard's purpose of exposing the emptiness of the chitchat while giving *The Switch* a nice comic touch.

The next novel Leonard wrote, *Touch* (originally called *The Juvenal Touch*), is an oddity among his work: not only doesn't it contain a single killing, its main character is a man with unusual, possibly even supernatural powers—he's a stigmatic, a man who bleeds from the same five wounds Jesus Christ suffered on the cross. A dozen publishers rejected the book when it was completed in 1977. Bantam finally purchased it, then stalled and never released it. It took ten years before it was finally published in 1987.

The novel tells the story of an ex-Franciscan brother named Juvenal who has come to Detroit after spending eleven years at a Franciscan mission in Brazil. He now works with drunks at the Sacred Heart Rehabilitation Center in Detroit. What makes Juvenal so unusual is his stigmata: periodically, his hands, feet, and side bleed mysteriously, and when they do he seems to have the power of healing. In the opening scene of the novel, for example, Juvenal visits the home of a drunken man who has become violent. He calms the man and then tends to his blind wife, whom the husband had punched in the face. After Juvenal finishes ministering to her, her face is smeared with blood, though she suffered no cut. And her sight is miraculously restored after fifteen years of blindness.

Naturally, Juvenal begins to attract attention. One person interested in him is Bill Hill. Hill is an ex-preacher whose church, the Uni-Faith in Dalton, Georgia once boasted The World's Tallest Illuminated Cross of Jesus, 117 feet high, with Jesus Saves spelled out in blue neon at the top. Hill's star attraction was a backwoods faith healer named Bobby Forshay, who drew huge crowds to the church. Now a recreational vehicle salesman in Detroit, Hill hasn't lost his eye for promotion; if he plays his cards right, he figures an experienced promoter like himself ought to be able to sell a phenomenon like Juvenal to the right TV show for at least a million bucks.

Someone else interested in using Juvenal for his own purposes is August Murray, self-proclaimed leader of a reactionary group seeking to return the Catholic Church to its traditional forms of worship. Murray figures a stigmatic would be useful in helping to publicize his new church devoted to the outlawed Latin liturgy. An unbalanced fanatic, he'll do just about anything—including murder—to further his aims.

At the center of all the scheming is Juvenal himself, a model of serenity. Though he differs dramatically from most of Leonard's other protagonists (he's neither a criminal, an ex-con, nor a cop), he shares one important quality with most of them: a cool acceptance of things as they are. Waking up one day and discovering that your hands and feet bleed like Christ's wounds can be an unsettling experience, yet Juvenal handles it calmly. He isn't sure whether his bleeding is a gift from God or a psychosomatically induced state. But he refuses to worry about it. "When you get right down to it," he reasons, "what difference does it make. . . . I accept it, that's all. Do I have a choice?"[16]

Though he's thirty-three years old, Juvenal has never experienced love, at least not romantic love (after all, he spent most of his adult life at a mission in Brazil): "I bleed from five wounds and heal people, but I've never been in love. Isn't that something?"[17] he remarks. That situation quickly changes when he meets Lynn Faulkner, a former baton twirler with Bill Hill's Uni-Faith Church, now a record promoter in Detroit. Hill recruits her to pose as an alcoholic and to check into Sacred Heart looking for treatment so she can learn more about Juvenal. But Juvenal sees right away she's faking; and just as quickly she begins to fall in love with him.

In *Unknown Man No. 89,* both Jack Ryan and Denise Leary were pretty savvy and experienced lovers. For her part, Lynn Faulkner is no babe-in-the-woods: she was married to a rodeo saddle bronc rider for nine years. But Juvenal is like a child discovering a new toy. There is a real innocence about him and a genuine joy in his discovery of love. The love that develops between him and Lynn adds a nice romantic touch to *Touch.*

Touch draws upon experiences from several different periods in Leonard's life. In the early 1960s, after leaving his advertising job with Campbell-Ewald, he wrote several educational and promotional films. His first effort was a recruitment film for the Franciscans entitled "The Man Who Had Everything." While shooting footage in Brazil, the producer of the film met a Franciscan priest named Father Juvenal who was working at a local mission. The priest was thirty, yet looked eighteen. The producer decided to use him in the part of a young man trying to decide if he has a vocation to the priesthood. He was brought to Detroit, where Leonard first met him.

Leonard was deeply impressed by the young priest. "This guy really had an effect on me," he said, "in his simplicity, in the way he touched people, in the way he accepted everybody. He was always so happy. He wasn't grinning all the time, but he was serene. Nothing seemed to affect him."[18] Though the real Father Juvenal was not a stigmatic, in most every other way he became the model for the hero of *Touch.*

In the early 1970s, the period when he was writing original screenplays, Leonard wrote a twenty-two-page treatment for a film entitled *Jesus Saves,* about a Georgia fundamentalist preacher named Bill Hill and his 117-foot illuminated cross. Hill's services featured performances by a nineteen-year-old baton twirler named Louly Falkner (who becomes Lynn Faulkner in *Touch*) and a backwoods faith healer named Lindell Reason. Leonard later wrote a full screenplay version based on *Jesus Saves* entitled *The Evangelist.* Though the script was never sold, much of this material was used as background for *Touch.*

Nineteen seventy seven, the year Leonard wrote *Touch,* was also the year he stopped drinking. His own experience with alcoholic treatment, which he had previously used in *Unknown Man No. 89,* once again plays an important role in his new novel. Leonard even incorporates a real person into the novel, Father Vaughan Quinn, well-known in Detroit as the director of the Sacred Heart Rehabilitation Center.

While the criminal features of *Touch* are secondary to other elements in the novel, they share certain similarities with the crime novels Leonard was writing during this period. The schemes of Bill Hill and August Murray to use Juvenal for their own profit resemble the kidnapping situations in *Fifty-Two Pickup* and *The Switch.* And while there are no murders in the novel, there is a gun, August Murray's .38 Smith and Wesson Commando, and there's no telling what he'll do with it.

Judged by the standards set by his other works, *Touch* is disappointing. The novel's bad guys don't have the frightening credibility of those in Leonard's best novels, and Juvenal lacks the darker side that Leonard's most interesting protagonists possess. Also, Leonard is usually a scrupulously realistic writer, yet here he attempts to depict a mysterious phenomenon that may well be supernatural in origin. The novel also includes some scenes that are uncharacteristically implausible (for example, Juvenal miraculously removes August Murray's body cast and heals the wounds he suffered in a fall from a balcony, all in front of a live television audience).

However, viewed as a fictional experiment and judged on its own terms (as of course it should be), *Touch* has its rewards. The novel reminds us of the possibility of the miraculous in our everyday lives; it emphasizes the importance of accepting things we cannot change; and it dramatizes the redemptive power of love.

With the exception of his westerns, Leonard's books have always been difficult to categorize. This is truer of no book more than *Touch*. Bantam purchased rights to the novel as part of a two-book deal that included Leonard's next novel, *Gold Coast*. (Bantam paid sixty thousand dollars for both books.) But the publisher couldn't figure out what to do with *Touch*. Though the novel was eventually set in galleys, Bantam still stalled. When Leonard objected to the cover, which inexplicably depicted a man levitating, Bantam claimed that changing the cover design would necessitate a year's delay before the book could be published. A year passed, and then another, and still the book failed to appear.

In 1985, after *Glitz* became a best-seller, Bantam developed a sudden new interest in publishing *Touch*. So did Leonard's current publisher, Arbor House. When Leonard dug out his original contract, he discovered that because Bantam had failed to publish the book within two years of its purchase, the rights would revert to him if he claimed them. He did. Then his agent, H. N. Swanson, offered to sell the book back to Bantam, which thought it owned it, and to Arbor House. Arbor House bought it for three hundred thousand dollars, ten times the amount Leonard had received a decade earlier. The ten-year delay may have been frustrating, but it turned out to be lucrative as well.

Despite his commitment to crime writing since 1974, Leonard wrote one more western novel. Marc Jaffe, head of Bantam books, liked westerns and offered Leonard twenty thousand dollars to write a new one. So in 1979, seven years after *Forty Lashes Less One* appeared, he published *Gunsights,* his eighth (and final) western novel. Originally titled *Legends,* the novel is both a tribute to the action shoot-'em-ups and, like Stephen Crane's "The Bride Comes to Yellow Sky," an elegy to the heroic western genre.

Spanning a six-year period from 1887 to 1893 and incorporating a large cast of characters, *Gunsights* contains plenty of action, including several standard western scenes: gunfights, jail breaks, stagecoach robberies, etc. The main action revolves around a familiar issue in Leonard's work: the battle fought by Mexican, Indian, and black settlers to preserve their land against the encroachment of the powerful LaSalle Mining Company of New Jersey. However, this issue simply serves as an excuse for a trio of characters to act out their heroic fantasies.

The main characters are Brendan Early and Dana Moon, two old buddies, and Phil Sundeen, their longtime antagonist. Sundeen originally appeared in *The Law at Randado,* where he led the local residents in a lynching of two Mexicans being held in the local jail for stealing some of his cattle. Sundeen is a tough guy hired by the mining company to get rid of the settlers, who now include Dana Moon and his wife. Caught in the middle is Brendan Early, Moon's buddy, who now also works for LaSalle.

Driven by personal loyalties, unsettled scores, and, like their ancient Greek epic ancestors, an opportunity to achieve glory on the battlefield, the three men head toward an inevitable final confrontation. The battle shapes up with Moon and Early and twenty of their men on one side facing off against Sundeen and over a hundred of his men on the other. Suddenly, events take an unexpected turn as Leonard reminds us that the glory days of the Wild West (and also the glory days of the western novel) are now over.

As the battle is about to begin, the scene becomes overrun with newspaper reporters and photographers anxious to record the event for their curious readers back east. They are joined by Colonel Billy Washington, a Buffalo Bill–type promoter who wants to sign both Moon and Early to star in his All-American Wild West Show. Then, as the battle is about to begin, it is a woman who unexpectedly decides the issue: Kate Moon shoots Sundeen when she sees him pull a gun on her husband. Following this less-than-heroic defeat of Sundeen, everyone else loses interest and goes home. The action is over. And so too is an entire era.

Leonard would return briefly to the western genre twice more. In 1982, he published a short story entitled "The Tonto Woman," a love story about a white woman whose face was tattooed by the Indians she lived with for twelve years and a man named Ruben Vega, a memorable character who was killed in *Gunsights* but brought back to life for this story. Three years later, Leonard wrote an original screenplay for a western film about a man named Duell McCall who is forced to go on the run after killing the manager of a mining company. Titled *Desperado,* it was telecast on NBC in 1987.

Despite these isolated efforts, Leonard was now fully committed to writing crime novels with a contemporary flavor. And it wouldn't be long before his reputation in his new genre would soar far beyond anything he had heretofore enjoyed as a writer of westerns.

1. Memphis, 1934. Leonard, age 9, with his sister, mother, and an unknown woman. Based on a Bonnie Parker photo from that period. *(Courtesy of Elmore Leonard)*

2. Oklahoma City, 1929. Leonard's first toy gun, age 4. He still has never owned a real one. *(Courtesy of Elmore Leonard)*

3. Washington, D.C., 1946. Leonard, age 20, back from Navy service in the Pacific. *(Courtesy of Elmore Leonard)*

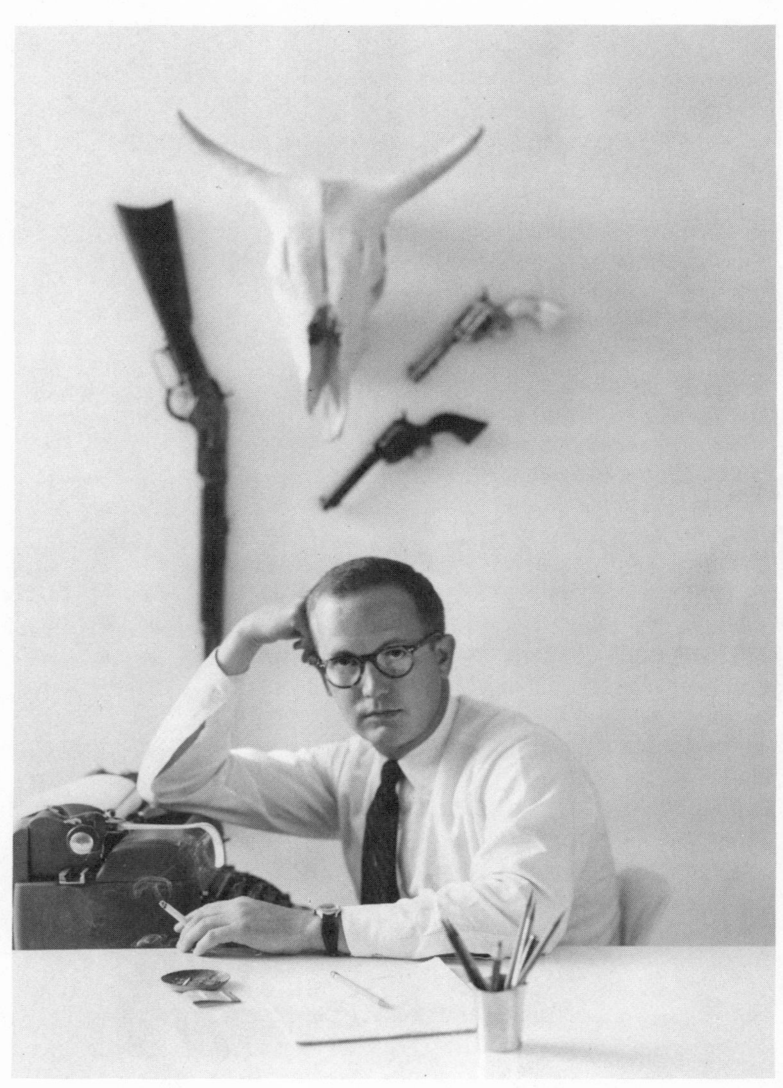

4. Leonard, early in his career. He began as a writer of Westerns. *(Courtesy of Elmore Leonard)*

5. Leonard at work at his writing desk.

6. Leonard in discussion with his researcher, Gregg Sutter. *(Courtesy of Gregg Sutter)*

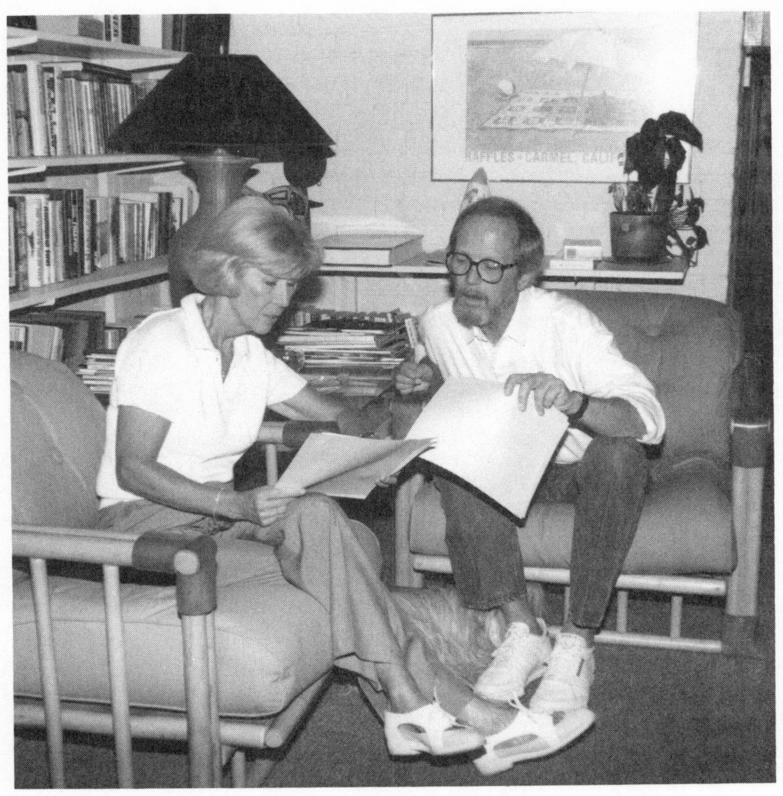

7. Leonard goes over his work with his wife, Joan. *(Courtesy of Gregg Sutter)*

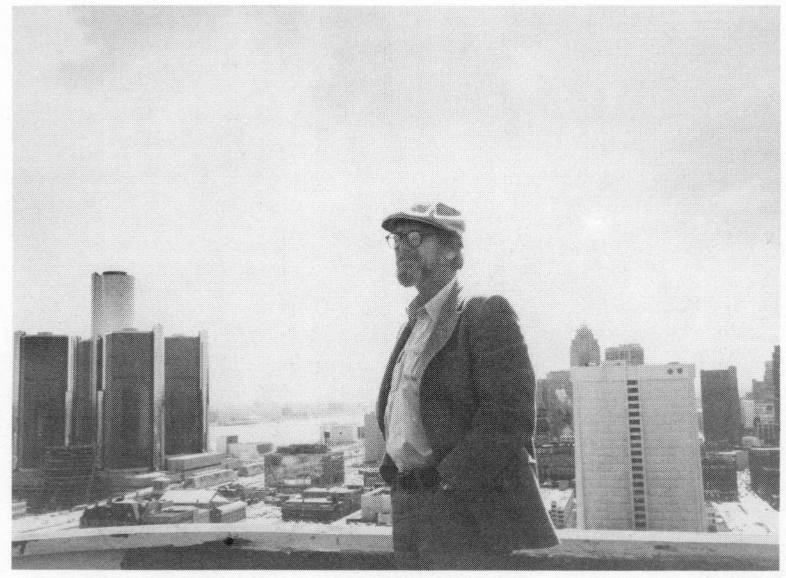

8. Leonard, with the city of Detroit in the background. *(Courtesy of Gregg Sutter)*

9. Leonard on location in Atlantic City, the setting for *Glitz*. *(Courtesy of Gregg Sutter)*

10. Leonard, autographing one of his novels. *(Courtesy of Elmore Leonard and Vagabond Books)*

5

Moving South: From Michigan to Miami

1980 was an eventful year for Leonard in that it saw the publication of two key novels: *Gold Coast,* his final paperback original, and *City Primeval,* his debut novel for Arbor House, the first publisher to market his works successfully. More importantly, both novels represent an advancement over his previous fiction and demonstrate his growing mastery of the crime novel.

Though *Gold Coast* appeared in December 1980, two months after *City Primeval,* it was written prior to that novel and sold to Bantam Books as part of the two-book deal that also included *Touch*. *Gold Coast* is the first of Leonard's novels to be set in Florida, which he had been visiting regularly since the late 1940s. It's also the first to benefit from his renewed acquaintanceship with college friend, Bill Marshall. The specific location for the action of the novel is Fort Lauderdale, home of John D. MacDonald's Travis McGee. Like the McGee books, *Gold Coast* features a damsel in distress, an ingenious financial arrangement, and a scary redneck monster; however, in Leonard's novel, there is no Galahad figure like McGee around to save the damsel from her menacing dragon. Leonard's victim has to fend for herself.

Though it is perhaps not entirely accurate to describe the forty-four-year-old, twice-widowed Karen DiCilia as a damsel, she is undeniably in distress. Her dead husband Frank was a Detroit mobster suspected, among other shady dealings, of being involved in the Jimmy Hoffa disappearance. When he dies suddenly of a heart attack, leaving her a million-dollar home on the Intracoastal, it would appear that she is set for life.

Husband Frank, however, was a fanatic on the subject of revenge. As he once explained to his wife, "I know all about paying back. I could write a book about paying back then look at it and realize I left a few things out."[1] It turns out he omitted nothing when it comes to paying Karen back for her discovery of his affair with another woman and threat to have one of her own: he leaves her a four-million-dollar trust that pays a quarter of a million a year; his will stipulates, however, that she must continue to live in his house and must never sleep with another man. To enforce Frank's final wishes, his lawyer recruits Roland Crowe to oversee the matter. But once Crowe learns that Karen is worth four million dollars, he schemes to get his hands on the jackpot for himself.

Crowe is both menacing and amusing. On the one hand, he's as scary as Bobby Leary, the homicidal maniac in *Unknown Man No. 89*. A former swamp guide, he now works as an enforcer for the mob. He once served eight years in prison for murder, though he committed several others for which he was never caught. ("If I notched my gunbutt you'd get splinters running your hand on it,"[2] he brags.) He's a tough guy who sure knows how to make a convincing point: to show a college kid who owes his employers $540,000 in a drug deal that went sour that he means business, he casually tosses one of the guy's buddies off the balcony of their fourth-floor apartment.

On the other hand, Crowe possesses some humanizing qualities: he loves animals (though that doesn't prevent him from killing a dog he likes when it becomes necessary), has a colorful way with words (he threatens one guy by telling him, "I take smartass little dinks that smell of fish and I tear 'em asshole to windpipe and throw 'em away"),[3] and a sense of humor in his choice of clothing (his underwear sports the slogan Home of the Whopper). He struts around, fancying himself a lady-killer, though the fact is he is simply a killer.

Eventually his path crosses that of Cal Maguire. We first meet Maguire during a holdup at the Deep Run Country Club in Bloomfield Hills, Michigan (the same club that figured prominently in *The Switch*): somebody wants to pay the club back for a slight and hires Maguire and two of his black buddies to do the job (only later does Maguire learn the man is Frank DiCilia, the revenge expert). Maguire and his partners get caught, but Maguire is freed on a technicality. It's time to leave Detroit, he decides. When his lawyer offers to get him a job at a porpoise show the mob owns in Florida, he heads for Fort Lauderdale.

But unlike Crowe, whose motives are obvious once he meets the very attractive Karen DiCilia and learns she is worth a lot of money, Maguire is more of a mystery. Given his background (nine arrests, no convictions) and his introduction in the novel as an armed robber, one is invited to have suspicions about his motives. But playing against the reader's expectations is one of Leonard's special talents.

The most surprising character in the novel, however, turns out to be Karen DiCilia, who proves she can take care of herself. Karen, one slowly realizes, is something of a risk-taker, which helps explain why a nice Catholic girl from Detroit like herself with an arts degree from the University of Michigan would ever become involved with a gangster. As a young girl she was fascinated by Virginia Hill, the girlfriend of such notorious mobsters as Frank Costello and Bugsy Siegel, whom she remembers watching during the televised Kefauver hearings in 1951. She often wondered what it would be like to be her. When the opportunity arose to find out firsthand what being married to a gangster would be like, she married Frank DiCilia. However, she never bargained on his old-fashioned sense of honor or his obsession with controlling *her* honor.

Though Maguire initially believes he must assume the role of Karen's rescuer, he eventually learns he is mistaken. Instead of rescuing her, he finds himself looking into the barrel of Roland Crowe's gun. Karen has to rescue him, which she does by pulling a gun from her purse and coolly shooting Crowe dead. Then, just as coolly, in the final line of the novel she dismisses Maguire from her life: "I enjoyed meeting you," she says curtly. "Now beat it."[4]

Karen doesn't undergo the dramatic transformation that events cause to occur in Mickey Dawson's character in *The Switch*. With Karen, it's more a matter of the reader's initially underestimating her. Only gradually does one recognize the true nature of the lady who, like many of Leonard's male protagonists, proves to be tougher than anyone gave her credit for being.

In *Gold Coast* Leonard is more expansive and relaxed in his storytelling than previously. He takes time to develop side plots and secondary characters to an unprecedented degree. A good example of this is his portrayal of Maguire's job at Seascape, the porpoise show. These scenes give the novel a convincing picture of real life that serves as an effective counterpoint to the violent criminal world Crowe inhabits. By mixing playful porpoises and deadly barracudas like Crowe together in one novel, Leonard creates a richer fictional world.

The novel also shows the strong influence of Leonard's film work on his fiction. *Gold Coast* is broken into ninety-three brief scenes, many with abrupt shifts of setting or mood between them. This gives the novel the kind of rapid movement one finds in a fast-paced film. Leonard also turns over virtually all the narration to his characters. With the exception of two brief authorial intrusions, the novel is presented entirely from the points of view of his characters, seven of them to be exact. This colorful variety of perspectives adds a richness of sound to the novel, one of the hallmarks of Leonard's best work.

Gold Coast was not only underappreciated when it first appeared, it was virtually ignored by reviewers. Fortunately for Leonard, the other novel he published in 1980 would enjoy a much happier fate and begin to earn for him the recognition that had heretofore eluded him.

City Primeval (1980) carried at his publisher's insistence the subtitle *High Noon in Detroit,* which only highlights what should be obvious to any reader of the book: though the setting is contemporary Detroit, the novel is an urban western, or what Leonard himself describes as an "eastern western."[5]

The main players in this gritty drama are Raymond Cruz, a Detroit homicide detective, and Clement Mansell, a killer known as the Oklahoma Wildman. Cruz is trying to gather evidence to arrest Mansell for the murder of a Detroit judge named Alvin Guy. He knows Mansell committed the crime but doesn't have enough evidence to nail him. The novel thus starts out as a police procedural, with Cruz and his fellow officers from Squad Seven of the Detroit Police Homicide Section working to build a case. However, it eventually turns into a personal dual, a man-to-man contest between Cruz and Mansell that builds inexorably to an urban version of the Gunfight at the O.K. Corral.

Leonard for the first time employs a policeman as protagonist. His choice of hero was a direct result of the assignment he accepted in 1978 from the *Detroit News* to write a nonfiction profile of the local police. He would spend several days a week just sitting in the squad room, observing the police in action. Occasionally, somebody would come in and ask, "What's Dutch doing here?" and the cops would say, "Leave him alone. He's listening."[6]

Raymond Cruz, thirty-six-year-old Detroit Police Homicide Lieutenant, is, like most of Leonard's heroes, quiet, cool, and very capable. "You don't let things bother you," one of his colleagues notes. "You observe, you make judgments and you accept what you find."[7] Also like a typical Leonard hero, Cruz is a pragmatist who disciplines himself to accept what *is:* "I don't expect to see something and then look and say, uh-huh, there it is. I try to look without expecting and see what's actually there."[8]

Yet there is another side to this hardheaded realist, one that involves a touch of self-romanticism. During a conversation Cruz has with Maureen Downey, a fellow police officer, about *The Gunfighter,* one of Cruz's favorite westerns, Downey observes that his mustache looks a lot like the one Gregory Peck sported in the movie. Cruz's laconic reply, "Kind of," suggests it's a resemblance he's aware of. Later in the novel, when Sandy Stanton, Mansell's girlfriend, also mentions that he reminds her of a young Gregory Peck, Cruz smiles. (His reaction when Sandy later remarks, "I thought Gregory Peck was cool . . . but I think you could give him some lessons,"[9] goes unrecorded, though it's safe to assume it's very positive.)

A female reporter interviewing Cruz for the *Detroit News* even accuses him of growing a mustache just so he would look like young Wyatt Earp. "You relate to that, don't you?" she charges. "The no-bullshit Old West lawman." Then she adds, "I'm not playing the role, you are. Like John Wayne or somebody. Clint Eastwood."[10] But however much Cruz may fancy himself as some kind of movie cowboy, it's going to take more than a Wyatt Earp mustache to defeat the Oklahoma Wildman.

Cruz may be the hero of the novel, but Mansell is the more colorful character. Like Raymond Gidre in *Unknown Man No. 89,* he's a redneck displaced to the big city. Unlike the laconic Cruz, Mansell is a man with many opinions and a colorful way of expressing them. For example, he describes a flowery sports coat as looking "like a camouflage outfit in the war of the fairies"[11] and calls disco music "goddamn goat-tit music."[12] There is also something almost endearing about a guy who sports a bright new tattoo honoring his mother, who was swept up by an Oklahoma twister and never seen again.

But it would be a mistake to underestimate Mansell; he's not called the Oklahoma Wildman for nothing. He's a dangerous daredevil whose idea of a good time is to lie on railroad tracks and let the train pass over his back. Through the years he has also accumulated an impressive crime record: by his own count, 266 stolen cars and nine murders, including that of Judge Guy.

Ironically, Mansell had no idea he was killing someone as important as a judge. The man he shot for bumping his car as he was leaving a Detroit area racetrack one evening was just "some spade with a little fag mustache."[13] Judge Guy isn't a particularly popular figure in Detroit, especially among the police (he once held Cruz in contempt of court for criticizing his harsh punishment of a twelve-year-old who acted up during a school field trip). Cruz doesn't intend to break his neck trying to catch the judge's killer. But once he determines that the killer is Mansell, he wants to nail him because of an incident three years earlier when Mansell beat a murder rap on a legal technicality. The police lost him on that one; now they have a chance to get even.

City Primeval is certainly no whodunit. Everyone, including the police, knows that Mansell killed the judge. Mansell also knows the police know he did it, but he also knows they can't prove it. The suspense arises out of the personal duel that develops between Mansell and Cruz. The two men develop a rapport that transcends their roles as cop and killer. "You don't set out to uphold the law any more'n I set out to break it," Mansell tells Cruz. "What happens, we get in a situation like this and then me and you start playing a game. You try and catch me and I try and keep from getting caught and still make a living."[14] Cruz responds, "Some other time—I mean a long time ago, we might have settled this between us. I mean if we each took the situation personally." To which Mansell adds, "Or if we thought it'd be fun."[15]

The inexorable buildup to a confrontation between the two bears a strong similarity to the situation Leonard described in *Gunsights*. In that novel, the personal rivalry between Phil Sundeen and Dana Moon also appears headed for a man-to-man shootout between the two. But in an unexpected ironic twist, Moon's wife pulls a gun and shoots Sundeen herself. Her action deflates the drama and emphasizes the point that the heroic days of the Old West have ended. *City Primeval,* however, makes the opposite point: i.e., that far from being over, the classic duals have simply moved from the deserts of Arizona to the streets of Detroit. The Old West may be gone, but there are still old-time gunslingers around to carry on its traditions.

In an afterword to *Gunsights,* Leonard observed that living in Detroit as he does would not at first seem conducive to the writing of westerns. "There sure aren't any buttes or barrancas out the window," he remarked. "But if you squint hard enough . . . you can see riders coming with Winchesters and Colt revolvers, and watch them play their epic roles in a time that will never die."[16] He just might have been describing *City Primeval* when he wrote those words.

Cruz and Mansell may be anachronisms, men born a hundred years too late, but *City Primeval* suggests that modern times still breed men like these. Detroit in the 1980s is shown to be a kind of lawless frontier. To begin with, even the sworn defenders of the law are less than honorable: the novel opens with a list of charges against Judge Guy, who has been accused of abusing his position and of ignoring the law. Then, when he and Mansell get into an altercation because his car cut in front of Mansell's, he expects the law to protect him: he intends to hold Mansell at gunpoint until the police arrive and arrest him for assault with a deadly weapon.

But Mansell has his own way of settling things: he opens the sunroof of his car, stands up, and shoots the judge five times with his Walther P.38 automatic while he's still sitting in his car. (For good measure, he also abducts the judge's girlfriend and later shoots her too.) Aside from demonstrating Mansell's violent nature, the scene also emphasizes the lawlessness of the streets.

The law is also shown to be powerless to deal with a crafty psycho like Mansell. Mansell admits to Cruz that he has committed nine murders; however, he has only been charged with murder once, and thanks to his clever lawyer Carolyn Wilder, he was freed on a technicality. Cruz is frustrated by his inability to charge Mansell with Judge Guy's murder, though there is no question that he is the guilty party. Sometimes it seems that it is only criminals like Mansell who benefit from the law by using it to foil the police in their efforts to nab them.

City Primeval contains an important subplot featuring a pair of Albanians, Skender Lulgjaraj and his cousin Toma. When Mansell became embroiled in the traffic incident with Judge Guy, he was hurrying to stay on the tail of Skender, whom (with the help of Mansell's girlfriend Sandy Stanton) he was planning to rob. After settling matters with the pushy Judge, Mansell eventually gets back to the Albanian. However, he becomes upset when he finds that

Skender doesn't have the large amount of cash on hand he thought he would. He takes his frustration out by breaking Skender's leg.

This brings Skender's cousin Toma into the action. To Albanians like Toma and Skender, personal honor takes precedence over civil or criminal law. If a man dishonors you, you kill him. It's as simple as that. Toma can't understand why Cruz can't just kill Mansell. "If you know he kills people," he asks, "why do you let him?" "It takes time," says Cruz. "No, it doesn't," Toma reminds him, "It takes only a few minutes."[17] Cruz finds himself divided between his professional obligation as a policeman sworn to uphold the law on the one hand and the temptation of Toma's simple, even simplistic, solution on the other. It comes as no surprise when Cruz decides, in the tradition of the Old West, to go after Mansell man to man.

With the help of Toma and Mansell's girlfriend, and with the tacit approval of Mansell's lawyer and one of his own police colleagues, Cruz maneuvers Mansell into Skender's secret soundproof basement room. Like Fortunato in Edgar Allan Poe's "The Cask of Amontillado," Mansell is imprisoned in his own tomb and left to die. However, this fails to satisfy Cruz's hankering for a more personal resolution to his duel with Mansell. So he quietly slips into Skender's basement, unlocks the door and then retreats to wait for Mansell to show up at his girlfriend's apartment.

Though he once said to Cruz, "Be something we had us a shooting match, wouldn't it?"[18] Mansell now isn't so sure he wants to duel it out with him. Cruz, however, has no intention of backing down. When Mansell reaches inside his jacket for what turns out to be only a bottle opener, Cruz shoots him. Mansell is finally brought to justice, frontier style. The novel ends with Cruz calmly paring his nails with the sharp edge of Mansell's bottle opener, which echoes Gregory Peck's action in a key scene from *The Gunfighter* described earlier in the novel.

City Primeval is given a rich texture thanks to the extensive research Leonard conducted while observing the Detroit Police Department close up. Leonard actually incorporated into his novel much of the material he used in "Impressions of Murder," (which appeared in the *Detroit News Sunday Magazine* on November 12, 1978). The murder charge Mansell ducked is based on an actual Detroit dope pad killing recounted in the opening of the newspaper article. The descriptions of the squad room in both the article and the novel are identical, down to the seven telephones, the Norelco coffee maker, and the hundreds of mug shots pasted to the wall. Even some of the dialogue is used in both pieces, including the remark made by a man whose girlfriend he and his buddy murdered after both had sex with her: "This is what I get," he complained, "for playing Mr. Nice Guy and *sharing* my broad with my buddy."[19]

Leonard had ever since *Fifty-Two Pickup* been devoting closer and closer attention to the sounds of his characters' voices. Now he had a rich new vein of material to mine that would add even greater realism to his fiction. The portrayal of the officers of the homicide squad, their relationships with each other and with the criminals they daily come in contact with, is convincingly authentic. Every scene in the novel has a sense of documentary realism about it.

Leonard sold the film rights to *City Primeval* to United Artists and was hired to write the screenplay (titled *Hang Tough*) himself. In 1981, Sam Peckinpah, the noted director of such western films as *Ride the High Country, Pat Garrett and Billy The Kid,* and *The Wild Bunch,* was selected to direct the film. Peckinpah flew to Detroit (where the film was to be shot) to meet with Leonard and scout locations. However, the project never proceeded beyond that stage and the film was never made.

City Primeval was the first of Leonard's novels to be published by Arbor House, which was owned by Donald Fine, Leonard's editor at Dell in the 1950s. Though Fine was the first publisher to promote Leonard effectively, *City Primeval* wasn't a big hit (for some reason, Newgate Callendar, the *New York Times* reviewer who had been singing Leonard's praises since 1974, even missed it). However, it wouldn't be much longer before Leonard's works finally began to reach a much-wider audience.

For *Split Images* (1981), his next novel, Leonard did something he had long resisted doing: he took the first step toward creating a series. At the encouragement of his publisher, he decided to bring Raymond Cruz back for a return appearance. This wasn't the first time Leonard used the same character more than once: Jack Ryan, for example, appeared in both *The Big Bounce* and *Unknown Man No. 89,* but those novels were separated by eight years and Ryan, an ex-convict, is no hero. This would be the first time he wrote back-to-back novels that featured a bona fide good-guy hero like Raymond Cruz.

Leonard's plan, however, hit a snag. His agent reminded him that he had already sold the film rights to *City Primeval* (and to the character of Raymond Cruz) to United Artists. A sequel would only complicate matters and make a film deal for *Split Images* impossible. So Leonard made a few minor changes in his main character: he gave him the same bandit mustache as Cruz, but changed the name of his ex-wife from Mary Alice to Peggy; he also transferred him from Squad Seven to Squad Five of the Detroit Police Department. Then he went through the entire manuscript changing the name Raymond Cruz to Bryan Hurd (though an alert reader will note that on p. 65 he missed one and the character still bears the name of Raymond).

Despite his plan to employ the same hero, it is clear that Leonard designed *Split Images* as a different kind of novel than *City Primeval.* He accomplished this mainly by shifting the setting for much of the book from Detroit to Palm Beach, Florida, and by creating new types of characters distinctly different from those in his previous book.

The villain of the novel is Robbie Daniels, a Detroit multimillionaire manufacturer. Unlike Clement Mansell, who is revealed as a homicidal maniac in his very first appearance in *City Primeval,* Daniels is a more subtle case. He, too, is presented as a killer in the opening scene of *Split Images,* but his action is judged justifiable homicide: he shot a Haitian intruder who broke into his luxurious oceanfront estate in Palm Beach. Later it is learned that nine years earlier he also killed another man, but that was apparently a hunting accident. But when Daniels cold-bloodedly guns down a parking lot attendant in the basement of the Detroit Plaza Hotel, the reader knows that here is another psychopathic killer like Clement Mansell.

Clement Mansell was a familiar Leonard character, the redneck displaced to the big city; Robbie Daniels is a different kind of character. A prominent industrialist worth $100 million, owner of a couple of million-dollar mansions and a fleet of luxury cars, he's very much at home in the wealthy environs of Grosse Point Farms, Michigan, and Palm Beach, Florida. No one meeting the boyishly handsome Daniels, who could pass for a movie star or a tennis pro, would ever suspect he's a killer. However, there are really two Robbie Danielses, and the one hidden behind the glamorous surface is the one Leonard is mainly interested in.

Daniels is a gun nut looking for an excuse to shoot somebody. The Haitian intruder provided him with an unexpected opportunity, but now he's after bigger game. Daniels believes that certain people deserve killing. He selects for his first victim wealthy Palm Beach playboy Chichi Fuentes, illegitimate son of former Dominican Republic dictator Trujillo. He says he targets Fuentes because he's a drug trafficker the police can't touch, though his real motive appears to be more personal: Fuentes snubs him by regularly forgetting his name.

Daniels is also a video nut. Both his homes are equipped with hidden cameras that secretly record whatever happens there. He loves watching videotapes; a special favorite is the one of John W. Hinckley's attempted assassination of President Reagan, which he views over and over again. Daniels finds an outlet for both his avocations after meeting Walter Kouza, a former Detroit police officer now working for the Palm Beach police. Daniels will kill Fuentes; Kouza will record the incident so Daniels can study it the way a football team reviews its game films.

That *Split Images* did not turn out to be the sequel Leonard intended to write was not his only surprise; another was the character of Walter Kouza, who started out as a bit player and ended up elbowing his way into the spotlight. Initially, the crusty veteran policeman was to appear in only the opening scene, where he was called in to investigate the shooting at Daniels's home. He wasn't even given a name, though he is described vividly:

Middle-aged stocky guy with short arms that hung away from his body. That shitty-looking thin hair greased back in a shark-fin pompadour the young cop would bet would hold for days without recombing. The guy sounded a little bit like Lawrence Welk the way he talked, not so much with an accent, but seemed to say each word distinctly without running words together. He seemed dumb, squinting with the cigarette in his mouth to get a half-assed shrewd look. But the guy did know things.[20]

But once he opened his mouth and began talking in his blunt, know-it-all manner, Kouza sprung to life. Leonard found himself with a character who demanded a much-larger role in the novel. "I gotta use this guy," he decided. "I gotta throw him in with Robbie Daniels. The contrast is beautiful with these two guys working together."[21]

So Leonard has Daniels invite Kouza in for a drink and some conversation. Daniels figures a veteran of nineteen years on the Detroit Police force like Kouza must know something about killing. He asks his visitor if he ever shot anyone. "I shot nine people," Kouza answers. "Eight colored guys, one Caucasian. I never shot a woman." How many did he kill, asks Daniels. "I shot nine, I killed nine," Kouza states proudly, though to clarify the record he adds:

They were all DOA except this one guy, a jig, hung on three hundred sixty-seven days, if you can believe it. So technically his death wasn't scored as a hit. I mean he didn't die of gunshot, he died of like kidney failure or some fucking thing. But it was a nine-millimeter hollow nose, couple of them, put him in the hospital, so . . . you be the judge.[22]

Daniels shows Kouza his collection of guns and asks him who he'd *like* to kill, anybody in the world. As the two of them sit there discussing various candidates, the reader might well wonder what's going on here? A veteran cop and a multimillionaire discussing potential murder victims? Are these good guys or bad guys? As so often happens in a Leonard novel, it will take a while to find out.

Leonard weaves an elaborate web to draw his characters together. The action begins in Palm Beach, then switches to Detroit, hometown of both Daniels and Kouza. Daniels returns to Detroit to oversee the sale of his manufacturing company, Kouza to appear in court for a suit brought against him by the mother of a youth he killed while he was a member of the Detroit police force.

Switching to Detroit enables Leonard to bring Bryan Hurd into the action. At first, Hurd's involvement is purely professional: he's called to court to testify about the strong-arm tactics Kouza employed when both were members of STRESS (Stop The Robberies, Enjoy Safe Streets), a controversial Detroit Police decoy unit that operated in the 1970s. (Of the twenty-two killings committed by nearly a hundred STRESS officers, Kouza racked up eight.) Then when Curtis Moore, another son of the woman who brought charges against Walter Kouza, is gunned down in the Detroit Plaza Hotel, Hurd is assigned to the case.

Hurd becomes personally involved thanks to his relationship with Angela Nolan, a free-lance writer preparing a profile of Daniels for *Esquire*. She and Hurd meet for the first time at Kouza's trial and before the day is over they end up in bed together. Angela provides Hurd with information that convinces him that Daniels is a primary suspect in Curtis Moore's murder. Then she provides him with a compelling personal reason for wanting to get Daniels: she has the tragic misfortune to be at Chichi Fuentes's home when Daniels arrives. After killing Fuentes, he kills her too.

The bloody scene at Fuentes's home is one of Leonard's best. The chapter begins lightheartedly enough, with Daniels worrying about what to wear to the shooting and Kouza grumbling about all the video equipment he has to lug through the woods. But as soon as the reader learns that Angela has chosen this time to interview Fuentes, the situation turns grim. Leonard keeps the reader off balance and the tension at an intense level by deftly alternating point of view between Kouza, who is videotaping the incident, and Angela, who is totally unaware of the dangerous situation she is in.

The killing of Fuentes goes as Daniels planned. However, the reader's relief that Angela had apparently safely escaped gives way to horror when the narrative switches to her point of view and follows her as she returns to the house from a walk along the beach. She arrives just in time to see Fuentes's body falling into his swimming pool. Once she realizes what is happening, she runs. The scene then switches to Kouza's point of view as he videotapes Daniels shooting at the fleeing woman. As soon as he recognizes that the woman is Angela, he drops his camera and leaves. He also leaves the reader in suspense: the chapter ends without the reader knowing for certain Angela's fate.

Her death isn't disclosed until the next chapter and the full horror of her murder isn't felt until the chapter after that, when Hurd is shown a videotape of the incident (dropped by Kouza when he ran off). The scene, recorded in icy silence by the camera, is chilling:

> He saw her eyes pleading. He saw her eyes close and open, her expression change, her mouth stretch open in a silent scream and saw the red splotch appear on the front of the white dress. He saw another red splotch and another red splotch and another red splotch and another red splotch and red strings coming out of those red splotches pulling her, yanking her off her feet.[23]

Leonard employed a similar device in *Fifty-Two Pickup,* where Harry Mitchell was shown the film of Cini Fisher being shot several times. However, this scene has greater emotional impact because unlike Cini, Angela is a character both the reader and Bryan Hurd have come to care deeply about.

A reader familiar with the dramatic final shootout between Raymond Cruz and Clement Mansell at the conclusion of *City Primeval* might well expect another "Gunfight at the O.K. Corral" confrontation between Hurd and Daniels. Leonard, however, seldom does the predictable; he chooses instead to end *Split Images* not with a bang but a whimper, though an appropriately ironic one.

Back in Detroit, Kouza attempts to sell Daniels a copy of the videotape he shot of Fuentes's murder. Instead of buying it, Daniels shoots his partner. When Hurd discovers Kouza's body in his Hamtramck home, he thinks he might have found a way to get his man. Hamtramck is outside his jurisdiction, so first he has to move Kouza's body inside the Detroit city limits. (In a nice touch, Leonard has Hurd deposit the body under the statue of Rodin's *The Thinker* in front of the Detroit Institute of Arts; earlier, when Daniels was trying to decide what to wear when he killed Fuentes, his pose reminded Kouza of the same statue.) Then he obtains ballistic evidence that proves that Kouza was killed with the same gun Daniels used to shoot the Haitian intruder. Hurd can now arrest Daniels for Kouza's murder.

Split Images is about murder, not robbery: the only theft in the novel is perpetrated by Walter Kouza, who steals the show. He's a cranky sourpuss with no sense of humor, yet every time he opens his mouth something funny comes out. Whether he's explaining his philosophy of life ("I haven't been surprised at anything since I found out girls don't have weenies")[24] or commenting on the murder of Curtis Moore ("Somebody was gonna do Curtis sooner or later. . . . What's the difference? Go down the morgue, see all the fucking Curtises they got there"),[25] he evokes laughter. A comic highlight of the novel is the narration he provides to a videotape he shot of a woman sunbathing in the nude.

Though a street-smart ex-cop, Kouza is naive about many things (which is part of his charm). He's never heard of actor George Hamilton (even after he meets him he doesn't know who he is) and he mistakes rock singer David Bowie for a girl when he sees a poster of him. He's never heard of Jodie Foster, the actress John Hinckley sought to impress by shooting President Reagan: his idea of the kind of woman to kill for is Norma Zimmer, one of Lawrence Welk's former champagne ladies. But in the case of Robbie Daniels, his naïveté isn't funny, it costs him his life.

One can laugh at the way Kouza dresses (his suits are always too tight, and he wears a raincoat over his pajamas instead of a bathrobe), at his sarcastic comments, even at his domestic situation (a killer of nine men, he's terrified of his wife). But he anchors the novel and provides a very human contrast to the calculated (and unfeeling) evil represented by Robbie Daniels.

Leonard continued in *Split Images* to draw upon material gleaned from his research with the Detroit police. He includes an entire chapter set at Detroit Police Headquarters. Angela Nolan accompanies Hurd to headquarters and watches as he and his colleagues begin their investigation into the killing of Curtis Moore. Presented from her point of view, the scene places the reader smack in the middle of the clatter of activities in the room: phones ring incessantly, a walkie-talkie squawks out numbers, a portable radio incongruously plays classical music, while several cases are discussed simultaneously. This vivid picture of police at work clearly shows why Leonard found his experience at Detroit Police Headquarters so fascinating.

Obviously pleased with the effects of research on his work, Leonard decided in *Split Images* to expand his methods by employing an outside researcher, a young Detroiter named Gregg Sutter. Leonard first met Sutter in 1979. Sutter later interviewed Leonard several times for a profile he wrote for *Monthly Detroit* magazine. In January 1981, as he was beginning *Split Images,* Leonard called Sutter and asked if he would be interested in doing some research for him. Sutter jumped at the opportunity.

Leonard asked Sutter to find out more about the Detroit Police Department's disbanded STRESS unit, which turned out to be perfectly suited to a cop like Walter Kouza. Sutter also provided Leonard with technical information about the hidden video surveillance system Robbie Daniels installed in his homes. He also drew upon his own experience working for an industrial auctioneer to provide background material for Daniels's automotive nuts and bolts factory.

Sutter also worked on Walter Kouza's background. Having himself grown up on the east side of Detroit, Sutter was familiar with nearby Hamtramck, a community settled (and still inhabited) largely by eastern European immigrants. He even found an area of torn-down buildings that served as the location for Kouza's childhood home.

For a scene describing Kouza's return to Hamtramck at the end of the novel, Sutter gave Leonard information about an actual Hamtramck bar named Lili's, a quiet neighborhood bar during the day, a swinging punk-rock hangout in the evening. Sutter composed an entire scene for Leonard for which he invented a punk-rock group he called The Pagan Babies. He even penned the lyrics for a song they sang while Kouza was at the bar.

What Leonard did with the material Sutter gave him offers an insight into his artistic methods. Leonard kept the bar, and even included Lili Karwowski, the actual owner, and her son Art, the bartender. But he took the scene Sutter gave him and completely redid everything from Kouza's point of view. Instead of hearing Sutter's lyrics, the reader gets Kouza's puzzled reaction to them, which is better. Not for the last time would Sutter express amazement at the way Leonard extracts exactly what he needs from what he is given, makes it entirely his own, and discards the rest.

Split Images has its flaws. The initial meeting between Bryan Hurd and Angela Nolan isn't entirely credible: there is no logical reason to explain her presence at Kouza's trial in Detroit, where she meets Hurd. Also, Daniels has enough weapons (and enough savvy) not to risk using the same gun to kill Walter Kouza that he used to shoot the Haitian, a mistake that provides the only possible way Hurd can get him for Kouza's murder. The relationship between Bryan and Angela develops fitfully, as if Leonard weren't sure exactly where to take it. And the lines he gives these two lovers to speak to one another (Bryan: "Are we in the neighborhood of what you want most?" Angela: "We're right there. I think we've always been there, but I have to feel it. You don't have to say a word if I feel it." "Start feeling,"[26] Bryan said) lacks the conversational brilliance of the rest of the dialogue in the novel.

But these are quibbles when compared to the many virtues of the novel: the brilliant characterizations, especially that of Walter

Kouza; the documentarylike portrayal of the police; the effectiveness with which Leonard captures both gray Detroit and sunny Palm Beach, cities that are literally and figuratively miles apart, yet that mirror each other as communities undergoing unwelcome change; and, as usual, the strikingly authentic dialogue.

Though Leonard's novels had been regularly earning good reviews (that is, when they *were* reviewed), none of his previous publishers promoted him very successfully. Arbor House was the first of his publishers to get behind him in a big way. For *Split Images* they purchased a full-page ad in the *New York Times Book Review* that featured excerpts from several of Leonard's best reviews, plus high praise from John D. MacDonald, who was sent an advance copy of *Split Images*. The ad also contained an enthusiastic (though not altogether unbiased) endorsement from Leonard's agent, H. N. Swanson: "I represented John O'Hara, William Faulkner, Raymond Chandler and Scott Fitzgerald all their lives for film and I consider Dutch Leonard to be in that class."[27]

Split Images didn't become a big seller, but it did garner excellent reviews, including Leonard's first mention in *Newsweek,* a rave notice by Walter Clemons. The highest praise of all came from Ken Tucker, who in the *Village Voice* proclaimed Leonard as "the finest thriller writer alive." Tucker suggested that Leonard is so good "primarily because he does his best to efface style," but added that because he manages to do this so effectively, "few readers know about him at all."[28] Larry Kart of the *Chicago Tribune,* who praised Leonard as "a very good, often inspired novelist whose subject happens to be violence and crime," also deplored Leonard's lack of a wider audience and announced:

> Reading a book as shrewd and powerful as *Split Images,* one wants to do what Eudora Welty did a few years back for Ross McDonald [*sic*] and what others have done (or tried to do) for John D. McDonald [*sic*], Dashiell Hammett and Raymond Chandler—somehow wrench the author away from those who merely absorb what they read and place him alongside those writers whose work rewards contemplation.[29]

Thanks to novels as good as *Split Images* and reviews as laudatory as these, it wouldn't be much longer before Leonard's work would finally achieve the recognition that people like Kart hoped it would.

Cat Chaser (1982) appeared only five months after *Split Images,* but it is definitely not a follow-up either to that novel or to Leonard's preceding one, *City Primeval.* In his new novel, there are no good-guy cops like Raymond Cruz or Bryan Hurd around to get in the way of the various bad guys. *Cat Chaser* presents an innovative treatment of a favorite Leonard situation: the scheming and maneuvering of a trio of con men and thieves to get their hands on another man's loot.

Patience is a quality Leonard's protagonists usually possess in abundance, and it is a quality a reader of *Cat Chaser* also needs. Unlike the situation in most of Leonard's books, the story in his new novel develops slowly. For the first hundred pages or so, Leonard appears unsure where he wants to go with his plot: he keeps introducing new characters and setting up several potential complications. But once things fall into place a patient reader will be rewarded with one of Leonard's most exciting stories to date.

The novel opens at the Coconut Palms, a twelve-unit resort motel in Pampano Beach, Florida, owned and operated by George Moran. Initially, attention centers on a Cuban piano player and his girlfriend who rent one of Moran's rooms for a daily afternoon love tryst. However, as the novel develops it turns out that the lovers simply provide an excuse to bring other more important players into the story: Nolen Tyner, an alcoholic ex-actor and part-time private eye who has been hired to find out who the woman is keeping company with; Jiggs Scully, a former New York City cop now working as an enforcer for a local mob outfit, who is hired by the woman to break up the affair; and Andres de Boya, a wealthy Dominican exile living in Miami, who is the brother of the woman in the motel room.

Leonard then discards the afternoon lovers and abruptly switches the scene to Santo Domingo. Moran decides to visit the Dominican Republic for sentimental reasons: he wants to locate Luci Palma, a sixteen-year-old sniper who shot at him while he was serving with the US Marines there during the US intervention in 1965. (His platoon was called "Cat Chaser.") He doesn't find Luci, but his trip serves to bring him in contact with two other key individuals. First, he runs into Mary de Boya, Andres de Boya's beautiful wife who has come to Santo Domingo to watch the polo. Moran and Mary, both originally from Detroit, have known each other for years; swept away now by passion, they become lovers. Moran also meets Rafi Amado, who assures him he can locate Luci Palma. But Amado is a con man; as soon as he learns that the woman Moran is having an affair with is the wife of Andres de Boya, a man well-known in Santo Domingo, he decides to try to blackmail the lovers.

Uncharacteristically, it has taken Leonard the first third of his novel just to introduce all his players, but now he's ready to heat things up. He returns the scene to Florida and then, halfway through the novel, introduces the element that sets everything into motion: Andres de Boya keeps several million dollars in cash stashed somewhere in his house. If James M. Cain had written *Cat Chaser,* Moran and Mary would conspire to murder de Boya and take his money and run. But Leonard chooses his own path: he links together Jiggs Scully, Nolen Tyner, and Rafi Amado and turns them loose after de Boya's loot.

This situation is similar to one in Leonard's 1969 novel, *The Moonshine War,* which described the efforts of a trio of thieves to steal Son Martin's moonshine treasure. At that stage in his career, Leonard was still celebrating the heroic qualities of the lone individual facing heavy odds against him. Now, however, he is more interested in the bad guys. De Boya isn't going to give up his money without a fight, but Leonard doesn't set him up as the hero of the novel. This shift to the point of view of the bad guys is one reason Leonard's fiction is so fascinating.

The first move on de Boya is made by Rafi Amado. Originally, he intended to extort money from Moran by trying to convince him that the young woman he brought to Florida with him is the dead Luci Palma's sister. But he's so obvious about his intentions that Moran doesn't bite. Nolen Tyner then enters the picture: he convinces Amado that de Boya is a much better target than Moran. But Amado is no match for Jiggs Scully, who uses both Tyner and Amado in his own plan.

To win de Boya's confidence, Scully informs him what Amado is up to. As former head of the *Cascos Blancos,* the Dominican secret police, de Boya knows how to handle threats against him (he reminds Moran of a "Latin Jimmy Hoffa"): he dumps Amado (who he knows can't swim) into his swimming pool and watches him drown. "That little spic makes a point he makes it, don't he?"[30] Scully later remarks to Moran, admiringly.

Moran declines Scully's offer to join him in his plan to steal de Boya's fortune. Moran's interested in de Boya's wife, not his money. Besides, he knows the cost of getting on de Boya's bad side: when de Boya learns that he has been sleeping with his wife, he sends a pair of sadistic goons to cut off his penis with garden shears and bring it back in a Baggie to his wife. Fortunately for Moran, they aren't successful. Scully will have to go ahead without him.

Like Walter Kouza, Jiggs Scully turned out to be another sleeper, a character who wasn't intended to play a major role in the novel but who was so colorful he took over. The two of them also share another trait in common: they are great talkers. Like Kouza, Scully utters the best lines in the book (a sample: "True love is beautiful," he counsels Moran, "but in seeking it you got to be sure and keep your nuts outta the wringer").[31]

Also like Kouza, Scully is an ex-cop. He now describes himself as a "business consultant," a go-between who brings people together who want to make deals, but in truth he's an enforcer for the mob (he works for Dorado Management, the same outfit formerly run by Karen DiCilia's mobster husband in *Gold Coast*). However, he's grown sick and tired of the "guineas and the spics" raking it in. "Something's wrong," he complains. "How come, I'm an altar boy, I go to mass and communion every morning of my young life, I end up working for the fucking guineas, the fucking spics, carrying their bags?"[32] He decides it's time to go into business for himself.

In *Split Images,* Leonard narrated large portions of the novel from

Walter Kouza's point of view, which kept the reader entertained by highlighting his sour outlook on things. In *Cat Chaser,* Leonard aims to keep the reader off balance more, so he rarely employs Scully's point of view. One sees Scully in action and is entertained whenever he speaks, but one never knows for sure what he's thinking. And one is never certain whom he's using and whom he's planning to double-cross.

Leonard displays great improvisational flair in *Cat Chaser*. First of all, in Jiggs Scully he has a character who, like Shakespeare's master villain Iago, invents his scheme as he goes along, turning incidents as they occur to his advantage. Leonard also plays a kind of shell game on the reader. While everyone is busy paying close attention to de Boya's suitcases, which everyone thinks are stuffed with cash, Leonard pulls a clever switch. Earlier, de Boya had kicked his wife out of their house when he learned about her affair with Moran. In a surprising twist, it is subsequently disclosed that before leaving, she packed her suitcases with her husband's cash and filled his with newspapers. It is she who ends up with the prize. If Scully wants it, he'll have to take it from her and Moran.

This revelation is preceded by another shocking development. Scully, de Boya, and de Boya's henchman Corky meet at an isolated farmhouse near the Fort Lauderdale airport. Scully is trying to maneuver de Boya into a position where he can snatch the cash everyone at this point thinks is in his suitcases. But de Boya is on to Scully's scheme. When Scully goes into the bathroom, de Boya waits until he hears the toilet flush, then opens fire at him through the closed door. But Scully (whose watchword is "Never take your joint out with guys you don't trust")[33] is too smart for de Boya. When Corky and de Boya push the door open, Scully is waiting for them. He herds both of them into the shower, and shoots them.

This scene reveals how Leonard works. When he began to write it, he himself didn't know who would come out alive, which of them would then have to go after Moran for the money. Who do I want it to be? he asked himself. If de Boya survives, he reasoned, all he'd have to do is torture Moran to get him to tell where the money is.

And what would Moran do? He'd tell him, Leonard decided, he didn't care about the money. "I figure it's gotta be Jiggs," he concluded, "because de Boya doesn't say that much. He doesn't talk. Jiggs, you couldn't shut him up. So he's the guy I want for the final scene."[34]

And the final scene is a dandy. Scully is an entertaining fella, but he's also proven to be a tough customer: he's already gunned down two men and delivered another to his death. If he has to, he'll kill Moran to get the money. But Moran is no pushover. In a scene that echoes the shoot-out between Clement Mansell and Raymond Cruz at the end of *City Primeval,* Moran outsmarts and outshoots Scully.

Scully should have known better than to tangle with the man whom he had once complimented by noting, "You're quiet, you mind your own business, don't you? Till somebody pushes you."[35] Though neither a copy like Raymond Cruz or Bryan Hurd nor an ex-criminal like Jack Ryan or Ernest Stickley, Moran is still very much a typical Leonard protagonist: cool in a crisis, tough when he needs to be. He's quite content running a small resort motel and minding his own business. But when his love for Mary de Boya forces him into a situation that he must handle well or die, he does what he must to stop Scully from taking her money.

As was becoming his habit, Leonard again did plenty of background research for *Cat Chaser*. He didn't have to go far to get material about running a resort motel. All he had to do was ask his mother: in 1969 he bought her a small motel in Palm Beach (also called the Coconut Palms) and frequently visited there. For background about de Boya, he had Gregg Sutter gather information about dictator Rafael Trujillo and also about the US intervention in the Dominican Republic in 1965. To get a better feel for Santo Domingo, Leonard even visited the Dominican Republic with his wife in 1982.

For information about guns and explosives, he called upon Sergeant Dale Johnston of the Detroit Police Department, a contact he had made during his research there. And he once again called upon former college classmate Bill Marshall, who had been regularly filling him in on the current Florida scene since 1977. (Leonard repaid the favor by naming the detective agency Nolen Tyner works for the Marshall Sisco Agency.)

But as was the case with his previous two novels, it is not the research itself but what Leonard does with it that matters. Certainly much of the background material he gathered for *Cat Chaser* wasn't needed for the novel; it wasn't absolutely necessary, for example, to have scenes set in the Dominican Republic, and the flashbacks to Santo Domingo in 1965 add little. What the research does, however, is help Leonard get a fix on things in his own mind. And it of course also adds texture, color, and flavor to the novel.

But as Gregg Sutter aptly notes of his boss, "he could write his next book in a sensory deprivation chamber, he has such an incredible imagination."[36] When it comes to creating lifelike characters, writing convincing dialogue, and constructing an inventive plot, research doesn't help. These elements come from Leonard's fertile imagination, not his research. These are what make *Cat Chaser* such an exciting reading experience, filled with satisfying twists, turns, and surprises right down to the final page.

"It has taken a little time," began Newgate Callendar in his review of *Cat Chaser* in the *New York Times Book Review,* "but Elmore Leonard is beginning to be taken seriously as a writer."[37] An understatement, to be sure, for it had actually taken Leonard over *three* decades and twenty novels to reach this point. But thanks to the growing maturity of his work and a promotional push by his publisher, his books were finally reaching a larger audience and a wider range of reviewers. *Cat Chaser,* for example, was lauded by everyone from rock publication *Heavy Metal* (which called the novel "an especial pisser")[38] to the more staid *New Yorker,* which proclaimed, "Mr. Leonard is a gripping writer—a really first-rate writer—and his moves, always plausible but much too fast to catalogue, are pleasurable in the extreme."[39] Though he wasn't yet a household name, the literary world was about to "discover" Elmore Leonard.

6

Fame and Fortune, Finally

One reason Leonard's fiction failed for so long to receive the critical and popular recognition it deserved was that it was difficult to categorize his books. His novels had no continuing main characters; they weren't private-eye stories, and despite the presence of an occasional police hero, they weren't police procedurals; most weren't even mysteries. What were they? Increasingly, it was becoming apparent that instead of trying to pigeonhole his works into one thriller category or another, it was time to recognize them for what they actually were: novels of character that often had as their subject crime and violence. None of his previous books makes this point more compellingly than *Stick* (1983).

Ernest Stickley, Jr., previously appeared in *Swag* (1976). That novel opened with him being interrupted by Frank Ryan as he was about to steal a car so he could drive to Florida to visit his seven-year-old daughter. This chance meeting resulted in a partnership with Ryan in a successful, albeit brief, career as an armed robber. But at the end of *Swag*, Stick's luck ran out and the cops nabbed him.

It's now seven years later and Stick has just been released from Jackson Prison in Michigan after serving a sentence for armed robbery. (Partner Frank Ryan wasn't as fortunate: he died in prison after drinking moonshine whiskey.) The novel opens, as *Swag* did, with Stick again on his way to see his daughter Katy, now fourteen. This time he finally makes it to Florida, but before looking her up he stops to see Rainy Moya, a friend from prison. Rainy talks Stick into coming along while he delivers a $200,000 cash payment from one drug dealer, Chucky Gorman, to another, Nestor Soto. Unbeknownst to Rainy, Soto has also demanded a life as payment from Gorman for what he considers Gorman's slipup in a drug deal. Gorman tells Soto to take Rainy's friend. Luck for once, however, is with Stick: Rainy gets the bullets meant for him. Stick runs for his life and escapes.

Though not a dumb guy, Stick has a knack for allowing himself to be drawn into troublesome situations; he also has a habit of ignoring what his common sense tells him he should do. If he had exercised better judgment seven years earlier, he wouldn't have gotten involved in armed robbery with Frank Ryan and he wouldn't have ended up in prison. If he had declined Rainy's offer, he would have avoided another close call. Now his common sense tells him to count his blessings and forget Chucky Gorman. But Gorman promised Rainy five thousand dollars to deliver the cash and Stick feels he is owed something for his troubles.

The more Stick thinks about it, however, the more sense it makes simply to walk away. He has just about decided to steal a car and forget Gorman when chance intervenes in his life once again. The owner of a gray Rolls Silver Shadow he has been eyeing approaches and, discovering he's locked out of his car, throws a fit. Stick, who has all the right tools handy, offers to break into the car and hotwire it for a hundred dollars. The owner, a wealthy Bal Harbour investor named Barry Stam, accepts Stick's offer. He also talks him into driving him home; by the time they arrive, Stick has agreed to become Stam's chauffeur.

His players now in position, Leonard can introduce his usual clever complications. Stick is surprised to learn that Barry Stam is a friend of Chucky Gorman; how, he wonders, can he use this unexpected piece of good luck to his advantage? But Leonard never settles for a single complication; Nestor Soto, unhappy that a witness to the shooting of Rainy is on the loose, orders Gorman to find Stick and kill him. Then there's Eddie Moke, a punk gunman who works for Soto; upset at Stick for crushing his new cowboy hat, he too wants him dead.

Leonard doesn't disappoint the reader who has come to expect crafty resolutions to his entanglements. Stick is given a big assist by Kyle McLaren, a whiz-bang financial advisor whose clients include both Chucky Gorman and Barry Stam. From her Stick picks up enough wheeler-dealer jargon and investment know-how to put together a scam that (if it works) will con Gorman out of much more than the five thousand dollars he believes Gorman owes him.

Though Leonard's plot is certainly ingenious, *Stick* is more than just another thriller: it is also a realistic portrait of a man attempting to overcome his past mistakes. At one point in the novel, Stick is reminded of Jack Henry Abbott, a convicted murderer who wrote the highly acclaimed *In the Belly of the Beast,* a collection of letters about life in prison. Thanks to the efforts of prominent supporters like Norman Mailer and others, Abbott earned his release. Six weeks later, however, he knifed a waiter to death in a minor disagreement over a rest room. Will Stick make a similar mistake and end up back in prison, a three-time loser? That's one of the main interests of the novel.

In many respects, Stick is the prototypical Leonard protagonist. For one thing, he's not a conventional hero: if you looked only at his record (two prison terms for armed robbery and four killings), you might conclude he's nothing but a hardened criminal. Yet though he's no saint, he's basically a decent guy who's had a run of bad luck. One of his main problems is that like a lot of Leonard's protagonists, he's overly passive. Instead of taking control of his life, he allows himself to drift into situations that cause him trouble. As he himself puts it, "I tend to get in the way of people who carry firearms."[1]

To his credit, Stick is also fundamentally an honest man, especially with himself. He makes no excuses for his past behavior. "I knew it [stealing] was wrong," he confesses. "And I knew I'd have to pay for it if I got caught. I accepted that."[2] While in Jackson, he insisted on wearing prison clothing (though he wasn't required to) because he wanted to remind himself that he was a convict; he wouldn't pretend to be something else until he got out. He insists on taking an objective view of things: "I look in the mirror," he declares, "I see what's there, nothing else."[3]

His criminal record notwithstanding, Stick isn't ordinarily a violent man. Of the four people he killed in *Swag*, two were attempting to rob him and the other two were planning to kill him. Only once in *Stick* does he employ strong-arm tactics (he wraps a telephone cord around Eddie Moke's neck in order to disarm him). He prefers to use his wits. This is brought out in the scene where he is confronted by the man he replaced as Stam's chauffeur. The man is drunk and very angry. Instead of fighting him, Stick fills a glass from a gasoline container, walks over to the man, splashes him with the contents of the glass, takes out a lighter, and asks, "You want to leave or you want to argue?"[4] Only later does one learn that Stick was bluffing—the container was filled with water.

As much as he likes Stick, Leonard doesn't make the mistake many authors do of falling in love with his hero. His aim is to humanize rather than lionize his protagonist. This is brought out the night Stick finds himself being invited into the beds of three very attractive women, one after the other. He services the first two, but in the case of the third, Kyle McLaren, the only one of the three he really cares about, he is unable to deliver. Stick, it turns out, is no sexual Superman. However, he's honest enough to acknowledge his failure and admit his mistake in seeking to include Kyle in his try for the sexual hat trick. On the basis of his actions, Stick may be no model of behavior, but in his honesty, self-awareness, and realistic attitudes, he's a man worthy of respect.

Leonard also isn't afraid to make his hero a loser in the end. After pulling off his enterprising scheme to con Chucky Gorman out of $72,500, Stick is in turn fleeced out of the money by his ex-wife Mary Lou: she has him served with legal papers ordering him to cough up $70,000 in delinquent child-support payments. Stick will have to settle for satisfaction at having engineered a successful scam, because he won't get to spend any of the money.

Stick is all about moneymaking. Money, of course, has played an important role in Leonard's previous books, but usually only insofar as it represented the jackpot everybody was angling to end up with. In *Stick,* money itself is the issue. To some, like big-time investor Barry Stam, money isn't something to be enjoyed; it must be put to work. "We sleep, you and I," he explains to Stick. "But money never sleeps, man. Play golf on the weekend, the money's still working its ass off."[5] He is one of those people for whom speculating, investing, and risking are more important activities than spending or enjoying.

But while money's working its ass off for people like Barry Stam, others are looking for a shortcut to the big payoff. For some, this means peddling dope; for Stick's fellow chauffeurs, it means selling their employers market tips they buy from Stick; for a shady Hollywood film producer like Leo Firestone, it means selling investors on a profitable tax fraud. Everybody's hustling to make a quick and easy buck, which often means breaking the law.

The $72,500 Stick cons out of Chucky Gorman is the thread that ties all these activities together. The money began as profits from selling drugs. Gorman then sought to launder the cash by investing it in Firestone's tax fraud. Stick intervened and diverted it into his bank account. Then ex-wife Mary Lou put in a legal claim for the cash. But in a final irony, the cash may well be headed for the pockets of a dental faith healer (who claims to fill cavities and correct overbites by the laying on of hands) who has already begun fleecing Mary Lou. *Shuck and Jive* is the name of the film Leo Firestone is trying to peddle to his prospective investors; it also describes the main activity of many of the characters in the novel. Everybody is conning everybody else, which only proves you don't have to stick a pistol in somebody's face to rob him.

What makes *Stick* especially effective as a novel is the way Leonard extends beyond the interest of mere plot. In part he manages this by exploring the potential of his setting. For the first time since he began using Florida in *Gold Coast,* setting becomes an integral element of the theme. It isn't topography, i.e., palm trees and picture-postcard vistas, that interests Leonard in *Stick;* it's the sociology of a place where the heady scent of easy money fills the air.

As Bill Marshall said of his old friend, "Dutch loves the beauty of Palm Beach and Fort Lauderdale, but he knows that those people on their yachts didn't all pay for them with the savings from their tire dealerships in Des Moines."[6] Leonard's Florida is as much a state of mind as a physical location, a place defined by greed as well as tropical greenery.

Leonard also in the novel adds more portraits to his growing gallery of unsavory villains: Eddie Moke, a punk Texas gunman who, depending on his mood, affects either a heavy-metal rocker image or a shitkicker image; Chucky Gorman, a psychological basket case who is usually so zonked on Valium and 'ludes it looks like he's wading through mud; and Nestor Soto, Gorman's drug supplier and practitioner of bizarre voodoo rites that involve chickens.

But the most interesting characters in *Stick* are only tangentially involved in the main plot. Chief among these is Kyle McLaren, Leonard's most successful female character to date. Ever since being criticized in a review of *The Switch* for his portrayal of women, Leonard has been working hard to make his female characters more believable and to give them more important roles to play. To this end, he admits having received considerable help from his wife, who offers suggestions and comments. The female characters in the novels after *Switch*—especially Carolyn Wilder, the lawyer in *City Primeval,* and Angela Nolan, the journalist in *Split Images*—have shown definite improvement.

Kyle McLaren is the mature result of that evolution in female characterization. Not only is she strikingly beautiful with a natural outdoorsy look, she is far and away the smartest character in the novel. She makes a very lucrative living researching investment opportunities and then advising a select group of clients where to put their money. She is the secret behind Barry Stam's fortune, though he gets the credit for being the market genius. Stick and the brainy investment expert come from different worlds, yet they find they relate together as man and woman quite well. Though romantic scenes (including romantic dialogue) are not Leonard's forte, the relationship between these two is handled more convincingly than some of his earlier attempts at such things.

Humor is always an important ingredient in a Leonard novel, and *Stick* is no exception. The novel is filled with clever one-liners and entertaining bits of dialogue. It also includes a pair of very funny guys. One is Barry Stam, a millionaire who fancies himself a stand-up comic, compulsively tossing off comic remarks à la Henny Youngman or Rodney Dangerfield. His jokes aren't particularly funny, but his desperate efforts to *be* funny are. His feeble attempts to play at being a tough guy are also comical. He likes to hire ex-convicts like Stick so he can show off by conversing with them in what he thinks is jailhouse argot, though when he tries to sound like a "hardass," he comes off sounding to Stick "like Eddie Fisher doing Marlon Brando."[7]

Leonard also gets a stellar performance out of Cornell Lewis, a black ex-convict who works as Stam's houseman. Aside from playing whatever role Mrs. Stam casts him in her bizarre sexual fantasies, he's also used as a kind of choric character who provides an entertaining commentary on life among the white folks like the Stams. Leonard is very effective in capturing Lewis's colorful language and disdainful attitudes as he plays his game of grin-and-chuckle with his employers.

Stick attests to Leonard's growing maturity as a novelist now confident enough to include scenes that are extraneous to the main plot, yet which add to the richness of the book. One such scene, a biting piece of satire, involves Hollywood producer Leo Firestone's attempt to peddle his idea for a new film to Barry Stam and a group of his wealthy friends. Firestone (known for a film entitled *The Cowboy and the Alien*) describes his new film as the hilarious escapades of a pair of undercover narcotics cops, though he's so dense he doesn't realize that most of his potential investors are drug dealers.

As he elaborates on his ideas about how to relate to the fourteen- to twenty-four-year-old audience and announces his cast (Erik Estrada, Neil Diamond, and Sir Lawrence Olivier in a cameo role),

Leonard pokes fun at the current thinking in Hollywood about moviemaking. Given his own Hollywood experiences, it's obvious that Leonard didn't have to rely on any outside research in order to write this scene.

The other scene is a domestic encounter between Stick and his ex-wife Mary Lou. After more than seven years, Stick finally makes it to Mary Lou's house in Pompano Beach. He's come to see his daughter, but he has to deal with his ex-wife first. The first words she speaks to him after all those years have an all-too-familiar ring to them: "Do you know what time it is?" she barks. The two are soon bickering like the unhappily married couple they once were.

Rehashing old complaints, Mary Lou relishes every opportunity to remind her ex-husband of his criminal past (i.e., "You going to give me the third degree now?" she asks. "You should be quite good at it, all the experience you've had").[8] The whole scene reads like one of those slice-of-blue-collar-life stories of contemporary marriage by authors like Raymond Carver or Bobbie Ann Mason, two of Leonard's favorite writers.

Stick was a turning-point novel for Leonard. Like his previous novels, it received excellent reviews, but he was now earning notices from those who didn't regularly review crime or mystery fiction, critics like Christopher Lehmann-Haupt of the *New York Times* and Jonathan Yardley of the *Washington Post.* (Yardley was so impressed that he lauded Leonard for raising "the hard-boiled suspense novel beyond the limits of genre and into social commentary.")[9] *Stick* also tapped into a new audience by being selected as an alternate by the Book-of-the-Month Club.

The novel also created a stir when it was sold to Universal Pictures for $350,000. Initially, Roy Scheider was to play Stick, but when Burt Reynolds agreed to direct as well as star in the film, the project was turned over to him. (Scheider would later give an excellent performance as Harry Mitchell in the 1986 film version of *Fifty-Two Pickup*). With a big budget and a major box-office star like Reynolds involved, Leonard had high hopes for the film.

The film, however, turned out to be a disaster. In June 1984,

Leonard was shown a preview of the movie, which was supposed to have been based on the screenplay he had written. At 6 A.M. the next morning he rose to compose a four-page letter to Reynolds detailing his objections, mainly about the direction of the film. Changes were subsequently made and some scenes reshot, delaying the film's release for several months. When it finally came out in the spring of 1985, the revised version was even worse. Asked his reaction to the film, Leonard responded: "I read somewhere that Bernard Malamud didn't leave his apartment for three weeks after *The Natural* opened—so I'm thinking maybe I should enter a Trappist monastery."

"It's just not what I wrote—not my book, not my screenplay,"[10] he complained. Melodramatic changes in the plot were made, scorpions and machine guns were added. The studio also insisted that the hero has to win, so the ending was changed to turn Stick into an avenger who settles everything with a smoking gun. In addition, the whole tone of the film is wrong. Leonard's lines, which demand to be read deadpan, were turned into jokes. "I do everything in my power to make my writing not look like writing," he said, "and when it appears on the screen you see all these actors acting all over the place."[11] There is so much mugging and smirking going on among the cast (which also included Charles Durning, George Segal, and Candice Bergen) that the title of the film ought to have been changed from *Stick* to *Shtick*. On the poster for the film he hung on his wall, Leonard made one correction: in the slogan used to promote the film—"The only thing he couldn't do was stick by the rules"—he replaced *rules* with *script*.

The widespread publicity surrounding the big movie plans for *Stick* had its bright side: Leonard was now becoming even more widely known. To take advantage of the situation, Arbor House decided to move the publication date of his next novel, *LaBrava* (1983), up by several months.

For a while, Leonard toyed with the idea of making his next book a sequel to *Stick*. First he considered putting Stick to work for a Florida private eye who hires him as a bodyguard for a female rock singer. This idea was dropped in favor of having Stick become involved in a new line of work, photography. But once the film rights to *Stick* were sold to Universal, Leonard, mindful of the problems he faced in trying to write a sequel featuring Raymond Cruz, abandoned the idea of using Stick again.

He did, however, retain the Florida setting and the photography angle for *LaBrava.* His new hero would be a Miami Beach photographer. But instead of employing a protagonist with a criminal background like Stick, he decided to go in the opposite direction: before taking up photography, Joe LaBrava spent nine years with the Secret Service. (Prior to that he spent three years as an investigator with the Internal Revenue Service.) Among his various assignments were guarding Teddy Kennedy during the 1980 presidential campaign and serving as a member of the detail guarding Bess Truman in Independence, Missouri. He first became interested in photography while doing surveillance work. The watchful eye he developed as a Secret Service agent is useful in his new line of work: he alertly spotted two men about to throw a third off a Miami bridge. The picture he snapped of the incident was so good *Newsweek* bought it.

LaBrava opens with Maurice Zola, eighty-year-old owner of the South Miami Beach hotel where LaBrava lives, asking him to come along while he retrieves a woman friend who has been picked up for public drunkenness. Zola wants LaBrava to take pictures of the woman so he can later use them, he hopes, to shock her into quitting drinking. But when LaBrava develops the film, he gets a jolt: he recognizes the woman as Jean Shaw, an actress he fell in love with twenty-five years earlier when he was twelve years old and saw one of her films. She is now over fifty, though she has lost little of that dark-haired beauty he still remembers so vividly.

LaBrava realizes that Jean Shaw is in some sort of trouble. His concern centers on Richard Nobles, a loudmouth troublemaker who was raising a ruckus at the Delray Beach crisis center where Jean was taken. Nobles is another of those redneck monsters Leonard enjoys using, like Roland Crowe of *Gold Coast* and Raymond Gidre of *Unknown Man No. 89*. "The Monster from the Big Scrub, with a neck so red it could stop traffic,"[12] is how Leonard describes him. He's a blond-haired giant with plenty of charm, a guy who knows how to use a "thin coat of syrup in his tone."[13] But he also has a reputation as a tough guy. When Jean Shaw receives a note threatening to kill her unless she forks over $600,000, LaBrava suspects that Nobles is behind the extortion.

It's too bad Leonard had already used *The Switch* as a title for a previous novel, for it would have made a perfect title for *LaBrava*. As he did with Andres de Boya's money-filled suitcases in *Cat Chaser,* Leonard again engages in some clever novelistic sleight of hand. All along LaBrava has been preparing to step in as Jean Shaw's rescuer. Halfway through the novel the reader is jolted by the disclosure that Jean Shaw is the one to be watched: she's the mastermind behind an extortion hoax that features herself as victim.

At this point one might feel a bit disoriented, which is exactly what Leonard intends. This isn't the first time the reader of one of his novels has been confused as to which are the good guys and which are the bad. Now that the victim has metamorphosed into the villain, one can't be certain what will come next.

Jean Shaw is a fascinating creation. She's no criminal, just an aging actress who discovers a way to play a starring (and profitable) role in a real-life script. In the sixteen films she made during the 1950s and 1960s, films noir with titles like *Nightshade, Shadowland,* and *Deadfall,* the dark-haired actress shared the big screen with such male stars as Robert Mitchum, Gig Young, and Victor Mature. She usually played the bad girl, the kind of woman who had her lover thrown off the Golden Gate Bridge *(Deadfall)* or who poisoned her husband *(Nightshade)*.

One of her favorite roles was in a film titled *Obituary,* a James M. Cain-type story in which she played a woman who conspired with her boyfriend (played by Henry Silva, who we are reminded also appeared in *The Tall T,* a western film based on one of Leonard's own short stories) to con her husband out of $150,000. But her husband proved to be too clever for her: knowing he was dying of an incurable disease, he committed suicide and staged it to look as if she killed him. In an ironic twist, she was convicted of murder and sentenced to prison for life.

Now, two decades later, Jean Shaw is retired and living in a luxury condo in Boca Raton. But she hasn't entirely forsaken her acting ambitions. She once wrote a script that she offered to Harry Cohn, head of Columbia Pictures. It was a story about a woman who cons a rich playboy out of a lot of money, even though he gives her anything she wants. That doesn't satisfy her, she wants to "earn" things herself. Cohn told her the idea stunk. Now she sees an opportunity to prove him wrong.

She assigns Richard Nobles and his friend Cundo Rey the parts originally played by Henry Silva and Elisha Cook, Jr., in a real-life remake of the hoax that was foiled in *Obituary*. Her intention is to swindle her longtime friend and benefactor Maurice Zola out of $600,000. Even though, like the playboy in her script, he is exceptionally generous to her (he's already given her $72,500 and his hotel is hers when he dies), she wants more independence. It isn't just the money she's after: she also wants an opportunity to star in her own story and to rewrite the ending to insure that this time she wins for a change.

Traces of Jean Shaw's character can be found in some of Leonard's previous female characters: like Nancy Hayes in *The Big Bounce,* she entices men into her criminal scheme; like Karen DiCilia in *Gold Coast,* she surprises everyone by being less a victim than she first appeared. But she is more complicated than either of these women. She isn't as deluded, say, as someone like Norma Desmond, the has-been actress in *Sunset Boulevard*. Jean Shaw hasn't lost the ability to distinguish between her film roles and real life. She's more like the character in Woody Allen's *The Purple Rose of Cairo* who steps down off the screen into real life.

Jean knows exactly what she's doing and enjoys her role, even when the script calls for her to commit murder. As an extortionist, she's just a clever amateur, but her acting experience allows her to fool almost everyone and reduces the Miami police and the FBI into unknowingly playing supporting roles in her script.

But her scheme fails to fool Joe LaBrava for very long. Having spent years eyeing suspects and examining thousands of threatening letters to the President, he can't help but be naturally suspicious. Especially when he keeps hearing Jean Shaw speak lines he recalls from her films. Even though he's had a crush on her since he was twelve years old, and lives out his fantasy by going to bed with her, he isn't taken in. But now that he knows she is mastermind rather than victim, what will he do about it? Will he turn her in? Or will he cut himself in on the jackpot?

Though certainly no conventional whodunit, *LaBrava* contains enough mystery to keep the reader riveted to the action. By refraining from presenting Jean Shaw's point of view, Leonard keeps one in the dark as to the specific details of her plan. Though it is known that she is in cahoots with Richard Nobles and that he has recruited Cundo Rey, a Marielito boat-lifter who now works as a part-time go-go dancer, the reader is never given the exact details of her plan. But whenever Leonard assembles a mismatched trio (which he often does), there arises the distinct possibility that one partner will double-cross the others. Add to this the uncertainty as to what Joe LaBrava will do and one has the ingredients for an intoxicating brew.

With so many possibilities, even Leonard himself wasn't sure how the novel was going to end. He saw three possible endings: Jean could get arrested; she could die; or she could end up with the money. His wife Joan, however, suggested a fourth possibility: foiled in her plan to con Maurice Zola out of $600,000, she could marry him and end up with the money anyway. Leonard loved the suggestion and used it to give the novel a nice ironic twist. To show his appreciation, he bought his wife a used Mercedes.

The scam that forms the backbone of the novel is just one part of a rich quilt Leonard weaves to give the novel its texture and color. The action is set against a fabric of authentic details comprised of information about Florida's past, about photography, about film noir, about the Mariel boat lift, about the Secret Service. To ensure factual accuracy, Leonard read books (Florida friend Bill Marshall gave him books like *Yesterday's Miami* by Nixon Smiley as well as a subscription to the Sunday *Miami Herald*) and old issues of magazines like *Holiday* and *Life*. He also talked to a photographer and to a Miami Beach detective about their jobs. Gregg Sutter provided plenty of information about one of his own passions, film noir. Getting specific information about the inside of Harry Truman's house presented a challenge; the Treasury Department wasn't very cooperative in providing details. Acting on a hunch, Sutter simply called information in Independence, Missouri, got the number for the house, then phoned the park ranger on duty, who described the interior of the house in detail.

Accompanied by Bill Marshall, Leonard also visited South Beach, an area that first caught his fancy when he was writing *Stick*. (It was the place where Stick hid out after Rainy was killed.) South Beach is an area of three- and four-story Art Deco hotels, "pale stucco in faded pastels, streamlined moderne facing the Atlantic from a time past."[14] Like Jean Shaw, these hotels are fading beauties that still retain plenty of their original charm. The guide through South Beach in *Stick* is Maurice Zola, a living link to the past, a rich storehouse of information about what the area was like before it became what he now calls "South Bronx south."

What gives South Beach its special flavor today is the striking contrasts in the area: to the population of retired New York Jews who originally settled the area has recently been added thousands of boat-lifted Cubans and Haitian refugees. (Leonard has always liked contrasts like this, going back to his early westerns, where he often wrote about the plight of the Indians facing the threatening arrival of the new white settlers into their land.) These disparate residents of South Beach live in an uneasy new melting-pot situation, each eyeing the other "with nothing remotely in common, not even the English language."[15]

Leonard uses the Florida setting differently in *LaBrava* than he did in *Stick*. In the latter book, Bal Harbour and Palm Beach, places where cash seemed to lie around in abundance, gave him an opportunity to develop the theme of moneymaking. In *LaBrava* Leonard isn't interested in relating crime to location as directly as he did in *Stick* (or in such Detroit novels as *City Primeval*). Jean Shaw's extortion scheme could take place anywhere. Setting in this novel is used simply as a realistic backdrop for a novel about people.

To enhance its realism, Leonard populates the novel with a wonderful cast of supporting characters: Mr. Fisk, an elderly South Beach motel owner who rebuffs Richard Nobles's attempt to force him to buy protection; Joe Stella, owner of the private security force Nobles sometimes works for; Jill Wilkinson, the spunky social worker at the crisis center where Jean Shaw is taken; Miney Combs, Nobles's uncle from the Big Scrub who has come south to settle a score with his nephew for snitching on his son; Johnbull Obasanjo, a Nigerian cab driver; Paco Boza, a Cuban who doesn't like to walk and thinks it's cool to pretend he's confined to the wheelchair he stole from Eastern Airlines. Though these characters make only cameo appearances in the novel, each one makes the most of his or her moment in the spotlight.

Franny Kaufman, an attractive young woman with frizzy hair, plays a larger role. She works part-time as a Spring Song girl who peddles skin creams and breast ointment to the aging ladies of South Beach. What she really wants to be is an artist, either a painter or a photographer. Though not involved in the plot, she does become involved with Joe LaBrava. If she served no other purpose than to describe what happens when she goes to bed with him, her presence in the novel would be worth it:

> "Oh Man. Man oh man." She said, "I bet there's a guy somewhere right now—he's in Boston, but forget what school it is—he's looking at a seismograph and he's going, 'Holy shit, look at this,' like he's got about a seven point five on his Richter and there's *got* to have been a major earthquake in the last five minutes or a volcano, another Mt. St. Helens, and this guy's seismograph is going crazy—a major disturbance, look, somewhere in Florida, and they narrow it down however they do it and the guy goes, 'Look, in South Beach. Ocean Drive and Thirteenth. Wait. Room two-oh-four, the Della Robbia Hotel. But what could it've been?' "[16]

When she gets to the end of her tribute (and the above is only a portion), LaBrava asks very simply, "You're saying you had a good time?"

The reader of *LaBrava* certainly has a good time. Though Leonard doesn't usually write what could be described as mysteries, *LaBrava* contains a greater proportion of mystery than usual in his books. In fact, it won an Edgar Allan Poe Award from the Mystery Writers of America as the Best Mystery Novel of the year. (It edged out such other worthy contenders as Umberto Eco's *The Name of the Rose* and John le Carré's *Little Drummer Girl.)* But *LaBrava* doesn't depend upon its mystery elements for its success. Like *Stick,* it is a realistic novel about believable people who become involved in an intriguing situation that occurs in a coloful location. The mystery elements may keep the reader reading, but it is the other elements of the novel that provide the greater satisfaction.

LaBrava brought Leonard to the threshold of fame and fortune. He was finally being "discovered." (Shortly after the novel appeared, the *New York Times* ran an article on Leonard by Herbert Mitgang under the ironic headline, "Novelist Discovered after Twenty-Three Books.") Winning the Edgar Award resulted in a major essay in *Time,* where J. D. Reed bestowed upon Leonard the impressive title, "A Dickens from Detroit." Later that year, Pulitzer Prize-winning author J. Anthony Lukas also profiled Leonard in *GQ,* where he was called "America's finest suspense writer."[17]

With fame came financial rewards. The paperback rights to *LaBrava* sold for $363,000; film rights brought $400,000. Not bad for a writer who began by selling stories for $100 and who was paid a paltry $1,250 for *Hombre,* one of his best-known works. For two decades, Leonard's film work had supported his fiction writing. Now his earnings from *LaBrava* alone could support him for the rest of his life. About the only prize he hadn't yet achieved was hitting the best-seller list, a situation that his next novel, *Glitz,* would rectify.

Leonard hit the jackpot with *Glitz* (1985). At the age of fifty-nine, thirty-four years after his first story was published, the momentum that had been building with *Stick* and *LaBrava* propelled him onto the best-seller list for the first time. (*Glitz* sold over 200,000 copies in hardcover, ten times *LaBrava*'s sales, and remained on the *New York Times* list for eighteen weeks.) The promise H. N. Swanson made to his client two decades earlier was finally realized; thanks to the $200,000 advance he received for the book (bumped up from $40,000 just before publication), the $450,000 he got for film rights, the $450,000 for paperback rights, and the $165,000 from the Book-of-the-Month-Club sale, Leonard was a rich man.

Glitz also sent critics scurrying to find superlatives strong enough to express their admiration for the novel: *Newsweek*'s David Lehman said, "Stylishly, and in a manner all his own, [Leonard] gives us the best the genre has to offer."[18] Christopher Lehmann-Haupt of the *New York Times* wrote: "*Glitz* is a jump to a higher caliber of entertainment. . . . You almost have to read it twice, the first time fast to find out what happens, the second time to savor it."[19] Chris Goodrich proclaimed in the *San Francisco Examiner* that Leonard "can no longer be considered a genre writer; in recent years he has become a master of the novel." *Glitz,* he argued, "demonstrates that Leonard is a better writer than most mainstream novelists."[20]

Some of the most colorful raves came from Leonard's fellow novelists. Stephen King, himself no stranger to best-seller lists, described *Glitz* as "the kind of book that if you get up to see if there are any chocolate chip cookies left, you take it with you so you won't miss anything."[21] James Crumley, in tune with the glitzy atmosphere of the novel's setting, wrote: "Each scene sparkles like a whore's sequined dress, each line of dialogue has the lower-depths authenticity of subway graffiti, and each slippery turn of the plot is both as surprising as seven straight passes with the dice and as inevitable as that final crap out."[22]

Glitz became a media event and Leonard a national celebrity. His face appeared on the cover of *Newsweek,* a rare honor for a writer. The accompanying essay contained Peter S. Prescott's previously-quoted statement naming Leonard "the best American writer of crime fiction alive, possibly the best we've ever had."[23] In his nationally syndicated column George Will likened him not to Dickens but to Anthony Trollope. *Chicago Tribune* columnist Bob Greene enthused: "Leonard is incredible. As a person who makes his living by trying to put words on paper, I am in awe of this guy."[24]

What unleashed this outpouring of superlatives strong enough to make a press agent blush? Actually, *Glitz*'s success was probably due more to timing than to any significant jump in quality. The momentum that had been building with Leonard's previous two novels now simply bore fruit. Aside from its settings—Puerto Rico and Atlantic City—*Glitz* isn't dramatically different from Leonard's previous novels. It's simply a new mix of standard Leonard features: a likable, low-keyed protagonist; an especially scary villain; a supporting cast of colorful secondary characters; great comic lines; plenty of plot twists; brilliant individual scenes; and a sense of accuracy down to the smallest detail, the product of Leonard's continuing reliance on research to get everything just right. In other words, Leonard simply did what he does best.

Ironically, *Glitz* happened by accident. After completing the *La-Brava* screenplay for producer Walter Mirisch, he was asked if he'd like to try his hand at a script for a sequel to *In the Heat of the Night*. The 1967 film starred Sidney Poitier as Virgil Tibbs, a black Northern police detective who travels to Mississippi and tangles with a redneck sheriff played by Rod Steiger.

Leonard began with the idea of having the Poitier character returning north, either to Philadelphia or Atlantic City. Leonard had become quite interested in Atlantic City and all its tacky splendor. He sent Gregg Sutter off to find out what was going on there. Sutter brought back such valuable sources of information as the *1983 Pennsylvania Crime Commission Report* on mob control of gambling in Atlantic City, plus some newspaper articles on organized crime in the area. "There are wild things going on over there," Leonard wrote Mirisch. "I know just from skimming what my researcher brought in there's my kind of book in it."[25]

The film deal eventually fell through when the studio that owned the rights to the Poitier character decided it didn't want to do a sequel. Leonard, however, continued to be interested in Atlantic City. He sent Gregg Sutter back to Atlantic City (Sutter's report of what he dug up for Leonard takes up eight pages of his *Armchair Detective* essay). In March 1985, he himself spent five days there, talking with the police and scouting out the casinos. Puerto Rico also presented itself as a possible setting "because it was a very, very cold day in Detroit and I decided Puerto Rico was a good place to go research."[26] He and Joan flew to San Juan, where he spoke with a former police superintendent. Now with a new hero (renamed Vincent Mora) and plenty of promising material, he had a novel to write.

Like many of Leonard's novels, including his westerns, *Glitz* is basically a revenge tale. Teddy Magyk, released from Raiford Prison in Florida after serving seven-and-a-half years for rape, vows to get even with Vincent Mora, the Miami Beach policeman who arrested him. He tracks Mora down in Puerto Rico, where he went to recuperate from injuries he suffered when a mugger shot him. Mora, however, has little trouble fending off Magyk's initial threat: with the help of a pair of Puerto Rican police friends, he scares him into leaving the country.

Two weeks later, Mora is summoned to Atlantic City by the police when his name and address are found stuffed in the panties of a dead woman, Iris Ruiz, a young Puerto Rican hooker he had befriended in San Juan. Iris, who moved to Atlantic City to work in a casino, was pushed to her death from the eighteenth floor of a condominium. Though Mora doesn't yet know it, this is Teddy Magyk's way of luring him to his hometown.

Teddy Magyk is Leonard's creepiest villain. Though he looks harmless ("He looks like a guy rings a little bell and sells ice cream," says Mora. "He walks down the street, you wouldn't give him a second look"),[27] he's a demented psychopath. He's served time twice for rape, the second time for an assault on a seventy-year-old woman. In *Glitz,* he commits three of the most brutal killings in all of Leonard's fiction: he guns down a Puerto Rican taxi driver, a father of four, because he was upset that the man looked at some photographs he took of Mora; he pushes Iris Ruiz off an eighteenth-floor balcony, then jokes, "An eight-point-five. . . . Nice execution, buy 'ey, she didn't keep her feet together";[28] finally he robs and brutally kills an elderly woman by bashing her head against the wooden support under the boardwalk; then he lights a match to examine her genitals before raping her. (When Vincent later asks him why anyone would rape an old woman who was already dead, Teddy replies, "Well, a woman like her can't be too choosy as to *when* she gets it.")[29] Even his mother's pet parrot gets edgy whenever he approaches his cage.

Leonard has a real talent for making his villains believably human, even one as twisted as Magyk. It helps him, he says, to picture his villains as children. In *Glitz,* he portrays Teddy as an overgrown child, a mama's boy. When not in prison, he still lives at home with his mother, upon whom he's dependent for money and for a car. Watching this cold-blooded killer trying to wheedle his mother into giving him more money exposes a side of Teddy that colors our reaction to him. He isn't made sympathetic, but he is made human.

Nothing demonstrates what one critic calls Leonard's "eerie ability to get inside empty heads"[30] better than his handling of Teddy's interior monologues. It's impossible to like Teddy, but Leonard forces the reader to view the world from his twisted perspective. One of the most disturbing scenes in the novel is his stalking of the elderly slot-machine player whom he intends to rob of her winnings. Through his eyes one watches as he lures his victim to her brutal death. What's so disconcerting about the whole affair is that Teddy acts like it's all his mother's fault because she won't give him any more money. Teddy is tempted to kill his mother, but he never will; he'll just find another elderly woman to rape and kill instead.

But revenge comprises only one element of *Glitz*. The novel is also a murder mystery centered around Vincent Mora's search for Iris Ruiz's killer. The reader knows long before Mora does that Magyk is the culprit, but that doesn't diminish interest in his efforts to get at the truth. Leonard has, of course, employed police heroes before, characters like Raymond Cruz and Bryan Hurd. However, this time he makes his hero a free-lance cop. He doesn't want a cop who is just doing his job; he wants one emotionally involved. Also, this way he avoids turning *Glitz* into a police procedural. Mora isn't bound by the restraints of legal procedure. As he explains to Atlantic City police detective Dixie Davies (who, by the way, is given the name of one of the real police officers Leonard befriended during his research stint with the Detroit police) before going off to question one suspect: "I wouldn't have to be as nice to him as you are, would I? Read him rights, anything like that."[31]

The cat-and-mouse game played by Magyk, seeking revenge, and Mora, seeking justice, is nothing new for Leonard. It formed the basis of both *City Primeval* and *Split Images*. A key difference between those two novels and *Glitz,* however, is in the extremes of good and evil represented by the participants: Teddy is a more frighteningly evil character than either Clement Mansell or Robbie Daniels and Mora is more the purely good guy than either Raymond Cruz or Bryan Hurd.

What makes Teddy Magyk such a chilling villain is that his victims are all innocents. They don't deserve to die. Also, Teddy's murders are all presented right before the reader's eyes (and, to make matters worse, presented from *his* point of view); nothing happens offstage, as it did in the case of many of Leonard's previous killers.

There are several reasons why Vincent Mora comes across as more of the hero-in-a-white-hat than his predecessors. One is that, unlike Raymond Cruz, he doesn't like to use his gun. He still hasn't gotten over having to kill the mugger who shot him in the opening scene of the book. He also has a streak of sentimentality his predecessors lacked: he returns the money to a café owner that a mob bagman extorted from him; he carries Iris's ashes all the way back to Puerto Rico to deliver them to her family; finally, all the trouble he goes through to avenge the death of a woman he hardly knew smacks of knight-errantry.

There is also more vulnerability to Mora, which Leonard brings out in several ways. For one thing, he's widowed, not divorced like most of Leonard's heroes. He's also shot twice, both times as he's helplessly carrying a bag of groceries in his arms. And the second time, his life is saved only by the timely intervention of a woman.

Like many of Leonard's novels, *Glitz* is also a love story. The novel offers several possible romantic partners for Mora: Iris Ruiz, the most beautiful woman Mora has ever met, and also the dumbest; long-legged but empty-headed beauty queen LaDonna Padgett; Nancy Donovan, the brainy woman who really runs her husband's casinos in San Juan and Atlantic City; and Linda Moon, a young piano player and lounge singer. Leonard originally planned to have Nancy Donovan play the key role with Mora, but once Linda Moon entered the scene, she took over.

Like Franny Kaufmann in *LaBrava,* Linda Moon is a free-spirited woman who says exactly what's on her mind. She's tough, independent, and ambitious. Though she has plenty of talent, she is often forced to mask it in order to accommodate her bosses' likes and dislikes. She's realistic enough to know she sometimes has to compromise (even to the extent of wearing a foolish-looking Chiquita Banana outfit), but she struggles to retain her self-respect and play her own music.

She's also very cool. When she prances naked out of Mora's bathroom and unexpectedly finds two other women in the room with him, she handles the embarrassing situation with enviable poise. She also has enough steely composure to resume lovemaking with Mora shortly after Teddy Magyk fires three shots into the room. Finally, she's gutsy enough to shoot Magyk herself in order to save Mora's life. "That Linda," Mora says respectfully, "you could put all your money on her."[32]

Setting his novel in Atlantic City affords Leonard an ideal opportunity to capitalize on plenty of colorful material. He's not a descriptive writer, so one gets little in the way of a pictorial image of the place. Instead, Leonard focuses on the people who work there (including some Mafia types), and those who are drawn there by the magnetic force of its gambling. The novel is also filled with atmospheric details, ranging from the incongruity of a note posted in Mora's room requesting that he turn off the lights when he leaves to conserve electricity, to a piece of helpful advice given by a man who spots Mora standing outside his hotel in his underwear (Mora was chasing after Magyk, who had attempted to shoot him while he slept): "You should a bet your underwear," the man advises. "You never know when your luck'll change."[33]

Leonard also incorporates material he assembled from his and Gregg Sutter's research. Mora's cooperation with the Atlantic City police in investigating Iris's murder offers a glimpse into the way the local authorities handle a murder case (this material is a product of Leonard's own conversations with the Atlantic City police). Mora's search for the killer also brings him inside the casinos, which enables Leonard to work in fascinating information about casino surveillance systems and the Eye-in-the-Sky monitoring of action on the gambling floor below.

Mora also comes in contact with a brilliant cast of characters: Jackie Garbo, the fast-talking head of casino operations at Spade's Boardwalk who prides himself on all his celebrity friends, whose autographed photographs adorn the walls of his office; his Ethiopian-born bodyguard, a former defensive end for the Miami Dolphins, who in a reversal of the usual practice changed his name from Moosleh Hajim Jabara to Deleon Johnson; LaDonna Holly Padgett, former Miss Tulsa Raceway, former Miss Oklahoma, an ex–Miss Congeniality whose fears about eating in Italian restaurants because gangsters are always shooting one another there prove to be justified; and a pair of homicidal gangsters named Ricky the Zit and Frankie the Ching.

From its opening line—"The night Vincent was shot he saw it coming"—*Glitz* unfolds dramatically. Like a fast-paced film, the novel contains 113 scene shifts. Point of view regularly shifts as the action moves quickly from place to place and from character to character. Leonard also experiments with point of view in order to get the best angle on a scene. For example, the action on the floor of the casino in one scene is described from the surveillance room, where observers monitor activities on TV screens, and in another from the observation area located in the ceiling.

Leonard often rewrites a scene to test how it works from a different angle. For example, a phone conversation between Jackie Garbo and a local mobster was originally presented as straightforward dialogue. Dissatisfied, Leonard decided to try the scene with DeLeon Johnson listening in on an extension phone. It worked much better, for in addition to information, the reader also gets a third-person reaction to the dialogue. Another example is the scene where Nancy Donovan chews out her husband and Jackie Garbo for allowing a Colombian drug dealer to launder money in the casino. When Leonard switched the point of view to Jackie Garbo and presented his reaction to being put on the spot by his boss, this scene also worked better.

The casino surveillance room contains a bank of twenty television monitors recording the gambling activities on the floor from a variety of angles. In *Glitz* Leonard is like a director sitting in front of all those screens, quickly cutting from one to another, giving the reader information while controlling rhythm, tension, and suspense. If he doesn't like the view from one camera, he switches to another. The result of all this point-of-view manipulation is a constantly shifting perspective that imparts a dynamic narrative energy to the novel. In *Glitz,* as in all of Leonard's best fiction, the story isn't everything; how that story is told is equally important.

Leonard's manipulation is so deft, so natural, that it is usually invisible. Only once does it become apparent. In an attempt at narrative symmetry, Leonard ends *Glitz* with a reenactment of the opening scene of the novel where Mora is shot through a bag of groceries (cool Linda Moon saves Mora's life by shooting Teddy Magyk, though the bullet passes through him and hits Mora). Although he was not consciously aware of it at the time he wrote the scene, Linda's action is also a reenactment of the final scene in *Gunsights,* where a woman with almost the same name (Kate

Moon) intercedes to shoot the man who is about to engage in a shoot-out with her husband.

Glitz was born out of an aborted film project. Then during the writing, it underwent several major changes (Nancy and Tommy Donovan, for example, were relegated to secondary roles once Jackie Garbo and Linda Moon made their presence known). Even the title was changed: Leonard originally intended to call the novel *Boardwalk,* but then discovered there was already a book with that name; when Swanson (who claims to have suggested *The Great Gatsby* to F. Scott Fitzgerald as the title for his famous novel) told him, "You'll come up with something with a lot of glitz and pizazz," Leonard thought, "That's it!"[34] He had his new title. Yet despite all the false starts, second thoughts, and alterations, *Glitz* turned out to be one of Leonard's finest novels. It stands as a testimonial to his confidence in following wherever chance, his creative instincts, and his characters take him. This time they took him to the top of the heap.

What do you do for an encore after a splashy success like *Glitz?* Leonard was so busy after completing that novel that he had little time to worry about his next book.

Even before *Glitz* appeared, he was busy working on the screenplay version of the novel. Then in August 1984, producer David Gerber signed him to write a screenplay for a pilot for a possible TV police series. Leonard had for a long time wanted to set a work in New Orleans, his birthplace, so he decided to use that city as the location for the film. He sent Gregg Sutter to New Orleans to begin gathering material, then visited it himself and talked with the local police. In November 1984, he completed the script for *Wilder,* a story about a New Orleans cop, which has yet to be produced.

A few months later, Universal TV also signed him to write a pilot. Producer Walter Mirisch, with whom Leonard had worked on several projects, suggested that he write a western (a pair of western films that year, *Pale Rider* and *Silverado,* had raised hopes that westerns would experience a comeback). In early 1985 Leonard completed the screenplay for *Duell McCall,* a story about a man on the run in the Old West. (Under the title *Desperado,* it aired on NBC in 1987.)

Leonard also spent a great deal of time on a frustrating succession of rewrites of the *LaBrava* screenplay to satisfy Dustin Hoffman, who finally approved the script and agreed to star in the film. However, the project fell apart when Hoffman later became involved in a dispute with the producers, Cannon Films. He broke his contract and backed out of the project.

By now Leonard had decided to set his next novel in New Orleans. He returned to the city to do additional research, and in the fall of 1985 finally began working in earnest on *Bandits* (1987). He had no intention of replicating *Glitz* either by using Atlantic City again or by employing a police hero like Vincent Mora. Instead, as was his wont, he tried something new. He employed a new setting (New Orleans) and created a fresh new cast of characters, including an ex-nun, a Nicaraguan colonel, a CIA agent, and an Irish Republican Army revolutionary. And for the first time he wrote a story that raised a controversial political issue, namely, American fund-raising efforts in support of the Nicaraguan contras.

Bandits began as a caper novel about a gang of old pros who get together for one last big score. For background research, Leonard visited the Louisiana State Penitentiary at Angola, where he spoke with veteran convicts. (He also took out a subscription to *The Angolite,* the prison magazine.) But somewhere along the way (long before the Iran-contra scandal broke), the idea of using the contras occurred to him, which changed his story and gave it a new dimension.

Jack Delaney is an ex–jewel thief who now works as an undertaker's assistant for his brother-in-law Leo Mullen. Lucy Nichols is an ex-nun who has left the leper hospital in Nicaragua where she had worked for nine years to return to her hometown of New Orleans. Jack and Lucy meet for the first time when she accompanies him to the leper hospital at Carville, where he has been sent to pick up the body of Amelita Sosa, a young Nicaraguan woman who died of the disease. However, it turns out that Amelita, a friend whom Lucy helped escape from Nicaragua, isn't dead at all. Lucy is attempting to hide her from Colonel Dagoberto Godoy, her former lover who wants to kill her because he believes she infected him with her leprosy when they made love.

Though a carload of Godoy's henchmen follow Delaney and try, unsuccessfully, to snatch Amelita from his hearse, *Bandits* is not a chase novel. Lucy tells Jack that Godoy is in the US to raise funds for the Nicaraguan contras. She also informs him that Godoy is a killer: he destroyed the leper hospital where she worked and murdered several patients. Lucy doesn't want Godoy to leave the US with any of the money he raises. She would like to use the money to finance a new hospital in Nicaragua; if Delaney helps her steal it, he can keep half.

Delaney enlists the aid of two former convict buddies: Roy Hicks, who used to be a cop before he went to prison; and Tommy Cullen, a master burglar who has just been released from prison after serving twenty-seven years. But *Bandits* is more than a caper novel. The scam is not the primary issue here as it might have been in one of Leonard's earlier novels; instead it serves as a vehicle for a treatment of two more important issues, one personal (the radical transformation of Lucy and Delaney), the other political (the US support of the contra war effort).

Like Mickey Dawson in *The Switch,* Lucy Nichols is changed by events that occur in her life; but unlike Mickey, who simply discovers the real "Mickey" under the false one, Lucy is engaged in a real search for identity. She decided to become a nun when, as a poor little rich girl of nineteen, she identified with Clare, the seventeen-year-old who 800 years ago fell in love with St. Francis of Assisi. As a young nun, Lucy prayed for a mystical experience (and also fantasized about levitating like her hero, St. Francis). However, her otherworldly inclinations did not prevent her from devoting herself to the down-to-earth task of ministering to lepers in a Nicaraguan hospital, which she did for nine years.

It was the atrocities committed by Colonel Godoy and his fellow contras at the hospital where she worked that began to radicalize her. Now back home in New Orleans, she gets the idea of stealing the money from Godoy to rebuild her hospital. "We're not bandits,"[35] she naively tells Delaney. She sees her plan as retribution, not robbery. But Delaney, the realist, knows otherwise: "If we're ever brought up," he cautions her, "don't be surprised if it's in criminal court."[36]

Though Lucy may be a romantic revolutionary, in the end, like all Leonard's heroes who are underestimated, she proves she has the right stuff. Roy Hicks declares he isn't going to stand by and let any nun take a million dollars back to a bunch of lepers in the jungle. When Lucy pulls a gun and threatens to shoot him if he attempts to take the money, he challenges her: "Sister, if you had the nerve, you'd deserve the money."[37] So she shoots him and takes the money.

Lucy is no one-dimensional character. She is a complex woman who is undergoing dramatic change. "I'm not the same person I was a year ago or this afternoon," she tells Delaney, "or the same person right now that I'm going to be."[38] Leonard paints a convincing portrait of a woman who trades religious fervor for radical politics, rosary beads for a pistol, and religious devotion for dedication to a cause.

Jack Delaney's conversion is less convincing. In the beginning he's totally apathetic about politics. While Lucy attempts to explain to him what's really happening in Nicaragua, he stares admiringly at her movie-star nose and fantasizes about biting her sexy lower lip. However, this, his first encounter with someone who "give[s] a shit about anything outside of themselves,"[39] miraculously transforms him into something of an idealist. He begins thinking in terms of helping "mankind." In the end he freely gives up his share of Godoy's loot to Lucy; he also even considers selling Godoy's sixty-thousand-dollar Mercedes, which has come into his possession, and sending her the money.

The problem is that Delaney, like most of Leonard's other protagonists, is too much the realist for that kind of sudden change. His willingness to participate in Lucy's plan is believable; it's easy to understand his attraction to her and to the prospect of a big score. Far less credible is his willingness to give up the money for the sake of "mankind." Leonard's protagonists often reveal a personal sense of honor; but not since John Russell in *Hombre* has any of them acted in such an honorable, selfless way.

A large cash jackpot is often the object of attention in a Leonard novel, but in *Bandits* the money plays a special role: the two million dollars raised by Colonel Godoy from wealthy private donors is more than just a jackpot to be stolen, it raises the whole issue of contra fund-raising itself. One of the highlights of the novel is a letter Godoy received from President Ronald Reagan, which is usually good for a check whenever he displays it to potential contributors. In the letter, Reagan affirms his desire to help Godoy "win a big one for democracy." Reagan adds that he hopes his letter will encourage "my friends in the Pelican State to give you a generous leg up, that you may ride to victory over communism."[40] (Leonard originally asked conservative columnist George Will, whom he met when Will interviewed him for a column he wrote about his work, if he wanted to write the Reagan letter. Will misplaced Leonard's request. When he finally responded several months later, it was too late; Leonard had already penned the letter himself, perfectly mimicking Reagan's characteristic style.)

Godoy's potential donors are wealthy right-wingers with a variety of personal reasons for supporting the contra war effort: if they are like Lucy Nichols's father, they are mindful of the tax benefits of a contribution; if they are like the Texas woman with $65,000 in cash to spare, they get to have a helicopter named after them; if they are like the fat cats attending a $500-a-plate dinner, they get to shake hands with a genuine contra, slap him on the back, and send him off with a rousing "Atta boy"; if they are like Alvin Cromwell, a gun dealer who dismisses the Klan as a bunch of "negative thinkers," supporting the contras is a way of fighting what he calls the dreaded "commonists."

Though tackling a political issue is a departure for Leonard, in at least one significant way *Bandits* resembles his other novels. Both

Jack Delaney and Roy Hicks wonder at different times just which are the good guys and which are the bad guys. In many of his previous novels, Leonard blurred the distinction between good guys and bad guys by making his heroes ex-cons who are thieves or even killers, and by making his bad guys very credible human beings.

In *Bandits,* this situation takes on political implications. Are the contras, whom President Reagan describes as the "moral equivalent of our Founding Fathers" and who are supported by well-meaning Americans and aided by a CIA agent named Wally Scales, the good guys? Or are they vicious killers who burn down hospitals and hack helpless patients to death with machetes? Leonard leaves little doubt about where he stands on this issue. (His indictment of the contra cause is underscored by the disclosure that Godoy is just a bandit himself who plans to keep all the cash he raised and head for Miami rather than Nicaragua.)

Bandits is not a political novel in the way that Robert Stone's *A Flag for Sunrise* is. Stone's novel much more directly examines the issue of US involvement in Central American affairs. (Although coincidentally, a leading character in Stone's novel is also a radicalized nun like Sister Lucy.) *Bandits* is not about Nicaragua, it's about Americans, some of whom (like Lucy's father) are shown to be financial supporters of a war they know little about.

The reviews for *Bandits* were mixed. Some judged it among Leonard's finest works; the reviewer for *Time,* for example, predicted it would "fill the land with the sound of pages turning."[41] But for the first time, there was a strong negative response to one of Leonard's novels. Much of the criticism was aimed not at Leonard's attempt at something more serious than usual, but at his failure to handle his material as well as he did in his previous work. One reviewer assailed the novel for its "flabby and repetitious writing, transparent characters and a seamless web of cliches."[42] Another declared that the writing was "positively blowsy," the dialogue "protractedly pointless" and the characters "sharply etched in cardboard."[43]

Some of the negative response can be attributed to a critical backlash, an inevitable reaction to the unbridled success that surrounded *Glitz*. *Bandits* has many virtues: it contains one of the best opening lines of any novel in recent memory ("Every time they got a call from the leper hospital to pick up a body Jack Delaney would feel himself coming down with the flu or something"); Tommy Cullen, the sixty-five-year-old master burglar who has just been released from prison, is an inspired creation. (After being cooped up for so long, he has only one thing on his mind, a woman. His description of his frustrated attempt to seduce a great-grandmother with a hearing problem is a gem of comic narrative); the novel possesses Leonard's usual sense of authenticity down to the smallest detail (one learns more about how to embalm a corpse than perhaps one wants to know); and the subject is as topical as the six o'clock news.

On the other hand, *Bandits* is also seriously flawed. For one thing, Leonard's attention to the political implications of Godoy's jackpot caused him to lose control over the maneuvering of Delaney and friends to steal it. Once the trio of bandits are gathered together, the action stalls. Leonard fails to come up with a plan for them to execute. Even Roy Hicks seems to sense the problem when he remarks, "We don't have enough of a plan to know if it won't work or even to figure the odds. We're feeling our way along, is all."[44] Only the timely intervention of Franklin de Dios, a Moskito Indian brought to the US from Nicaragua by the CIA, resolves Leonard's plot dilemma. He shoots Godoy and steals the money himself when he concludes Godoy intends to keep it all.

Another problem is that several of the characters in the novel are abstractions rather than flesh-and-blood individuals. As a villain, Godoy is a personification of evil rather than an evil presence, like Teddy Magyk. There are stories about his atrocities, but Leonard never convinces the reader he's dangerous. Wally Scales is a CIA agent whose business it is to know what everybody is up to. But his purpose seems limited to establishing the behind-the-scenes role played by the CIA. Give Leonard credit for timeliness and prescience, for *Bandits* was written before the Iran-contra scandal hit the news and the extent of the CIA's involvement under Director William Casey became known. But like Godoy, Scales never really comes to life on the page.

One character who definitely does come to life is Jerry Boylan, an Irish Republican Army agent blessed with the gift of gab. Delaney meets Boylan when both happen to break into Godoy's hotel room the same evening. (There are three such unexpected late-night hotel-room encounters in the novel, at least one too many.) Boylan is in New Orleans looking to get his hands on the contra arms for his own revolutionary effort. But then, without warning, he is shot in the back of the head by Franklin de Dios while visiting the rest room.

Boylan's death highlights an important feature of Leonard's fiction: in his novels, violence is usually sudden, shocking, and straightforwardly presented. One will rarely find detailed descriptions of violence in his books. "I don't see any need to glamorize it," Leonard explains. "When you shoot someone in the head, that's enough. . . . It's such an awful thing in itself that you don't have to adorn it in any way."[45] Letting violent acts speak for themselves delivers a powerful punch in Leonard's fiction.

Boylan's abrupt departure from *Bandits* is disappointing. Thematically, he serves the purpose of stirring Lucy's revolutionary fires. She becomes more committed to her cause after meeting him. But then he's gone. Leonard created Boylan because he wanted to try out a new sound. He had even done research by taking notes during a visit to Dublin. But when he ran out of Irish material, he decided to kill off Boylan, which may not be the best reason, from a thematic point of view anyway, for dismissing a character.

Bandits lacks the dynamic energy and narrative verve of *Glitz* and the well-rounded tightness of *Stick* and *LaBrava*. However, it's only by comparison with Leonard's previous successes that *Bandits* suffers. The fact that it falls short of his usual high standards is as much a tribute to the excellence of his best work as it is a criticism of this novel.

Bandits is as up-to-date as the daily newspaper. *Freaky Deaky*

(1988), by contrast, is an updating of yesterday's news. Its subject is not the making of a radical, as *Bandits*'s was, but rather the current activities of a group of ex-radicals from the sixties and early seventies.

In many ways *Freaky Deaky* is a return to basics for Leonard. The novel employs several familiar features—a Detroit setting, a Detroit cop as hero, several familiar faces from the squad room in *City Primeval,* including a cameo appearance by that novel's hero, Raymond Cruz, and an old-fashioned caper plot. However, there's nothing stale or familiar about the results, thanks to Leonard's ability to create fresh characters and his utter mastery of the storytelling art.

Like so many of Leonard's novels, *Freaky Deaky* began as something quite different from what it ended up as. It started as a story about a female singer whose car is blown up by the Mafia. She hires a suspended Detroit cop as her bodyguard, and the two of them fall in love. But at that point, nothing more happened, the story stalled. "I didn't feel I had enough room to roam around in and let things happen,"[46] Leonard said.

Then he began thinking about the guy who blew up the car. He contacted Dale Johnston, a member of the Detroit Police force whom he had used as a source of information before. Johnston, an explosives expert, gave him a book on how to make bombs. Leonard was fascinated by the material. It struck him that a guy who grew up learning to make bombs back in the 1960s was far more interesting than some Mafia guy connected to the record business. So he started researching that period and reading the stories of ex-radicals who went underground. *Freaky Deaky* quickly began to take shape.

Robin Abbott and Skip Gibbs are, like many of Leonard's characters, ex-convicts. What's unusual about their case is that their crime was political: each served three years for blowing up the army recruiting office in the Detroit Federal Building in 1971. It's now the late eighties and the radical days are over for most people. However, though she currently spends her time writing romance novels under the name Nicole Robinette, they aren't over for Robin.

Robin is looking for revenge. She blames the Ricks brothers, Mark and Woody, former radical friends at the University of Michigan, for turning her and Skip Abbott in. (They had jumped bond after their arrest and were living underground when they were arrested.) The Ricks brothers are now prominent citizens in Detroit. Mark is a theater producer who was featured in a *People* magazine article entitled "Yippie Turns Yuppie." His productions are financed by his brother Woody, an alcoholic who controls his mother's fortune, now close to $100 million. Though Robin isn't exactly sure how she's going to do it, she intends to force one of the Ricks brothers (she isn't sure which one) to pay her and Skip for all that time they spent in prison.

Like Nancy Hayes in *The Big Bounce,* Robin is a thrill seeker looking for a way to factor some excitement into her scam. Like Lucy Nichols in *Bandits,* she's a rich girl turned revolutionary. But unlike Lucy, whose radicalism seems more genuine, a product of her firsthand experience of war in Nicaragua, Robin's radical activities were always tinged with a certain amount of showboating. ("You gonna tell me we were trying to change the world?" Skip says. "We were kicking ass and having fun,"[47] he reminds her.) Her desire to rip off the Ricks brothers has nothing to do with politics. She's not out to tweak the establishment but to settle an old score. And in the process, to score a big jackpot.

Robin's partner, Skip Gibbs, is a bomb expert. Since his release from prison, he has been using his explosives know-how as a special-effects expert who blows up cars for the movies. But he's ready for more serious work. Robin knows how to entice a man like him into playing a key role in her replay of the past. Still sporting a beard and a ponytail, Skip is, like Robin, caught up in nostalgia for the good old days in Ann Arbor. But Robin also remembers Skip's fondness for acid, which she gives him as a way of insuring his participation in her plan. "Dynamite and acid, man," Skip exclaims, "that'll Star Trek you back to good times. The way it was."[48]

Bombs also provide our introduction to Chris Mankowski of the Detroit police bomb squad. *Bandits* has a memorable opening line, but *Freaky Deaky* has the best opening scene in all of Leonard's work. Mankowski is called to the home of a notorious drug dealer named Booker, who received a phone call from a girlfriend asking him to sit down by the phone; when he does, she informs him that when he attempts to get up, he will be blown to bits by the bomb he's sitting on.

Since this is Mankowski's final day on assignment with the bomb squad, he isn't eager to do anything that might get himself blown up. He especially doesn't want to risk his neck for someone like Booker. When Mankowski's partner arrives, the two of them nonchalantly walk away, leaving Booker sitting impatiently on his bomb. Strolling outside the house, the two cops light up cigarettes and chat about the buds on the trees. Mankowski begins to tell a story about his girlfriend when suddenly the windows and doors of Booker's house shatter in a violent explosion. Without missing a beat, Mankowski continues his story. The reader knows he is definitely in the company of another of those cool characters Leonard likes so much.

Mankowski shares a similar background with the other principal figures in *Freaky Deaky:* He was a student in Ann Arbor at the same time as Robin, Skip, and the Ricks brothers; he participated in the march on Washington, and went to Woodstock. But he also went to Vietnam, where he suffered serious injuries in a grenade blast. Now he's one of the "pigs" radicals like Robin used to protest against. Mankowski doesn't want to relive the past; he just wants to do his job, which will prove to present problems for Robin and her big Payback Scam.

A second stumbling block is Donnell Lewis, another figure from the past. Donnell is an ex–Black Panther who met Robin and Skip at a fund-raiser Woody and Mark Ricks's mother hosted in the early seventies for the Panthers (she thought she was raising money for the zoo). Fifteen years later Donnell bumped into Woody Ricks, now a full-fledged lush, and saw a golden opportunity: ever since then he has worked for the man whom he patronizingly calls Mr. Woody as chauffeur, cook, advisor, usually even as his brains. There is nothing altruistic about Donnell's watchfulness: he's simply biding his time, waiting for the right opportunity to take a big slice of Woody's fortune.

Robin is almost as clever as Jiggs Scully in revising plans and coming up with new schemes when old ones are thwarted. But Donnell, whom she recruits in a clever scam to con Woody out of two million dollars, is also a master at manipulation. This produces a familiar Leonard situation: a trio of partners (Skip Gibbs is still in the picture as the powderman) whose individual members' self-interest raises the distinct possibility that somebody is going to get double-crossed.

Leonard avoids turning *Freaky Deaky* into a standard cops-and-robbers story by having Chris Mankowski get suspended from the police force. (Woody Ricks's well-connected lawyers have him canned for arresting Woody on a rape charge.) Leonard likes to use cops, but he avoids Joe Friday types who are only doing their jobs. Like Bryan Hurd and Vincent Mora, Mankowski is a cop who gets emotionally involved in the case: he develops a personal interest in Ginger Wyatt, the woman Woody Ricks raped; more importantly, when Mark Ricks is blown up in an explosion that destroys Woody Ricks's car, Mankowski himself becomes a suspect in the bombing because it is known that his encounter with Woody Ricks caused his suspension. His role in the novel is thus colored by some question marks: is he after justice? does he just want to clear his name? or is he also interested in scamming some of Woody Ricks's money?

How Leonard brings together all these figures from the past and intertwines the various cons that arise is masterful. There are no loose ends in *Freaky Deaky*. Leonard integrates everything into a complex network of relationships among all his characters and keeps the action moving at a satisfying pace right down to the explosive conclusion to the novel.

Leonard has also never mixed crime and comedy together any more effectively than he does in *Freaky Deaky*. Crime is never treated lightly in his novels; nevertheless there is usually plenty of humor, both in the dialogue and in the characters.

As the man with the moneybags, Woody Ricks is the object of all the criminal maneuvering in the novel. But as a befuddled alcoholic who can barely function, he's also the butt of most of the humor. Leonard constantly ridicules his loutish behavior. When he's not doing something disgusting in public (like pulling a chair up to a buffet table and stuffing food into his mouth from the serving dishes), he floats in an alcoholic haze on a rubber raft in his indoor pool or numbly watches tapes of Busby Berkeley movies while smoking grass and gulping martinis.

Ordinarily, Leonard's characters define themselves through their dialogue, by what they say and how they say it. Woody doesn't say much (he's usually so out of it that what he might say wouldn't make much sense anyway), so everyone else takes a crack at describing him. His brother Mark calls him "the immovable 250-pound moron";[49] Robin describes him as "sort of an offensive Poor Soul";[50] Wendell Robinson, a Detroit policeman, jokes that he "has a wet brain."[51]

The funniest put-downs come from Donnell Lewis, the guy who has to nurse Mr. Woody through the day. "The man always in low gear with his dims on,"[52] says Donnell. Later he remarks that his boss "had chicken lo mein for brains" and observes that "if the man was any dumber you'd have to water him twice a week."[53]

Donnell is a rich source of humor in the novel. Like Walter Kouza and Jiggs Scully, he's a real scene-stealer. It isn't only what he says that is funny; his whole attitude toward things around him (especially Mr. Woody) is amusing. (In his role as comic commentator he closely resembles Cornell Lewis, the black houseman who works for Barry Stam in *Stick*. The similarity of their names makes one wonder whether they might perhaps be related.) The scenes involving him and Woody are among the funniest in the book, especially those that describe his daily struggle to get his boss out of bed in the morning and his prodding to get himself included in Woody's will. If scenes like these had been described straightforwardly, there would have been nothing special about them. But by presenting them from Donnell's point of view, Leonard colors everything with his contemptuous and irreverent attitude toward his dim-witted boss.

Leonard keeps himself fresh as a writer by trying out new sounds and new points of view. In *Freaky Deaky* this can be seen in those passages written from the perspective of characters whose perceptions are distorted in some way. For example, Leonard describes Skip Gibbs's experience during an acid trip; later he describes Ginger Wyatt's reactions after she is given some acid without her knowledge; finally, he gives us Woody Ricks's point of view (the only time he does so in the novel) as he awakens from a drunken sleep to terrifying visions of naked toads dancing in his alcohol-sodden head. While none of these scenes is absolutely necessary to an understanding of the characters, each provides further evidence of Leonard's uncanny ability to get inside his characters' heads.

In a career that has now spanned close to four decades, Leonard has produced an impressive body of work: twenty-six novels, eighteen of them crime novels. *Freaky Deaky* is not the culmination of his career, only the latest in a long line of highly original crime fiction. The novel proves that Leonard is writing at the top of his form: his mastery of his craft shows no evidence of abating, and his enthusiasm for his work remains high. Leonard's characters are often losers, but novels like *Freaky Deaky* are sure winners.

7

"Why Is Elmore Leonard So Good?"

Novelist Walker Percy spoke for many readers and critics alike when in his review of *Bandits* in the *New York Times Book Review* he concluded: "[Leonard] is as good as the blurbs say."[1] But Percy was also one of the few to ask the key question: "Why is Elmore Leonard so good?" Attention has often centered on Leonard's long-overdue rise to popular and critical acclaim after decades of obscurity. However, little effort has been made to explain the reasons behind the artistic excellence of his work. In large part this is due to the seeming artlessness of his novels. As Donald Westlake put it, "He's so good, you don't notice what he's up to."[2] But seeming artlessness is not artlessness. Fiction, no matter how natural it appears, is created, and in Leonard's case, created by an artist with rare gifts.

Leonard's literary excellence is the result of artistic genius coupled with an approach to writing that can be expressed in three main tenets: (1) Get It Right; (2) Let It Happen; (3) Be Natural.

1. GET IT RIGHT: For Leonard this means doing research. Research has played an essential role in his fiction since his earliest westerns. Often the purpose of the research is simply to gather specific information: how do the local police investigate a killing? how does a drug dealer launder money? how does a casino surveillance system work? how do you make a bomb? Research of this type enhances the realism of the fiction by insuring authenticity down to the smallest detail.

Leonard is not the sort of writer (like James Michener, for example) who does an enormous amount of research and then tries to incorporate as much of it as possible into his novel. He uses only what is appropriate, and what he uses he works in very unobtrusively. The factual information is never allowed to impede the flow of the story. A reader of *Bandits,* for example, won't be given every detail about how to conduct an embalming (which, based on his eyewitness research, Leonard could give); but because Jack Delaney is a mortician's assistant, the reader will be given enough details to convince him of the authenticity of the scenes of him at work.

What Leonard's research does for *him* is even more valuable: it provides him a clear picture in his own mind of his main characters. He will often develop an entire history of a character before beginning to write. His characters then become as lifelike to him as real people. Even if much of this background information is never included in the novel, it nonetheless gives Leonard a vivid feel for his characters. An illustration of how real his characters are to him is that he was prompted to write *Stick* when a glance at the calendar reminded him that Ernest Stickley, whom he had used seven years earlier in *Swag,* was due to be released from prison and he wondered what he was up to now.

In this process of familiarization, names are very important. "I love names. I can't get a character to talk until he has the right name,"[3] Leonard admits. (He also has a liking for certain names: there are multiple Ryans, Majestyks, Moons, Rendas, and Lewises in his novels.) *Bandits*'s Jack Delaney, for example, began as Frank Matisse, but for the first hundred pages or so he wouldn't talk very much. When Leonard changed his name to Jack Matisse, he opened up a little. When he finally became Jack Delaney, he came fully to life.

More important than getting the name right is getting the character's sound right. If there is any one quality that sets Leonard's novels apart from the works of most other contemporary writers, it is this, his remarkable ability to capture the sounds of his characters.

Leonard is a great listener. He possesses what one critic calls a "Panasonic ear"[4] capable of recording the exact sounds he hears.

Leonard doesn't use a tape recorder. When he listens, he isn't listening for specific dialogue but for rhythms of speech and cadences of sound. He has a particular liking for a certain sound. "It's the sound of savvy people, or people who *think* they're savvy and talk that way. To me, they're so much more interesting than educated people. . . . I guess I'm still a kid on the corner of Woodward Avenue listening to my friends, who were all blue-collar kids."[5]

Leonard is also a great transcriber. He is able to reproduce on the page what he hears so exactly, so true to life, that his writing sounds not so much written but, in the words of one critic, "as if it had been wiretapped."[6] He even fooled the Detroit police who were the subjects of the profile he wrote for the *Detroit News*. "They swore all the lines in it were tape-recorded," Leonard said, "which none of it was."[7] What he relied on was his ability to get their sound exactly right. Though he sometimes uses specific lines he picks up from TV or that are given to him by his wife and others, almost all his dialogue is made up. It just sounds real.

The range of sounds he captures is impressive. He is a true virtuoso of voices. Whether it's a black man from Detroit, a Moskito Indian from Nicaragua, a redneck from the Florida swamps, an ex–beauty queen from Oklahoma, a Marielito boatlifter, a revolutionary from Ireland, or even Ronald Reagan himself, Leonard creates a distinct voice. He only uses words—be they racist, obscene, or ungrammatical—that are appropriate to the specific character. Also, he follows the rules of grammar his characters do. A line like the following—"You mean like Sea World, they put on the porpoise show, a guy rides a killer whale, Shamu?"[8]—may not follow the rules of proper syntax, but that's exactly how some people really talk. What Raymond Chandler said about Dashiell Hammett applies just as well to Leonard: "He put these people down on paper as they were, and he made them talk and think in the language they customarily used for these purposes."[9]

Leonard does much more than simply mimic dialects. Getting the sound right enables him to expose the way his characters think. Once they open their mouths, they open their minds to us. Leonard prefers using multiple points of view rather than limiting himself to first-person narration (which he used only once, in *Hombre*). This frees him to employ a variety of sounds as well as a variety of interior monologues. He uses these monologues to express a character's thoughts in his or her distinctive language. Leonard never has to describe his characters; they reveal themselves.

Much has been made of the Elmore Leonard sound: tough, deadpan, funny. But the term "Elmore Leonard sound" is a misnomer. It's never his voice one hears, only the sounds of his characters. Leonard is a skilled ventriloquist whose own lips never move. He always remains in character, maintaining the sounds of his characters throughout the entire novel. There are similar voices in some of his novels simply because there are certain types of characters he enjoys using: cops, ex-cons, smooth-talking con artists, guys trying to sound tough. But there are always distinctive new voices to give a fresh sound to each book.

Leonard's uncanny ability to impersonate so many different characters demands great empathy on his part. He finds it helps to imagine all his characters, good and bad, as human beings; his heavies have to face many of the same problems (what to wear, when to eat, how to get along with their wives or mothers) that his good guys do. "The only premise I begin with is that my characters are human beings," Leonard says, "and I'm going to treat them honestly, despite their inclinations—not approving of those who commit criminal acts—but rather accepting the fact impersonally, without making moral judgments."[10] One reason his bad guys are so convincing is that they are treated with such understanding.

Leonard's good guys and bad guys are just ordinary people. His antagonists sometimes have good qualities; his protagonists, who are no storybook heroes, are sometimes even criminals themselves. By alternating point of view between the hero and the villain as he often does, Leonard further narrows the distinction between the two. Because there is no controlling authorial voice in the novel, both points of view are given equal time, so to speak. This has the effect of forcing the reader to relate to both on a common human level. Leonard doesn't expect the reader to overlook the actions of his bad guys; but demonstrating that it is real people who perform such awful deeds contributes to the potent realism of his fiction.

2. LET IT HAPPEN: Once Leonard begins writing his book, he switches to an entirely different approach. Instead of depending on research, he now relies on instinct. To borrow a phrase uttered by several of his characters, Leonard's philosophy of composition can be described as "letting it happen." As intimately as he knows his various characters, he never knows in advance what they'll do. Once he begins a book, he lets them "tell" him what will happen next.

"I hate to plot,"[11] Leonard concedes. He used to plot out his books very carefully; in fact, some of his early novels were based on detailed screenplay treatments he had first written. Now he no longer worries about plot. He knows one will take shape once he creates interesting characters and comes up with a situation that forces them to rub against each other. (He also concedes it is useful to have a gun somewhere in his story. "I don't have any desire to fire guns," he says, "but they come in handy in a book.")[12]

Leonard likes unpredictable characters; an unplotted story affords him a greater opportunity to take advantage of such characters. Also, not plotting his books in advance insures that the action will be natural and unforced. In many instances, Leonard doesn't know what will happen more than a scene or two ahead. Usually he doesn't even know how his novel will end until he is almost finished writing it. (The ending of *Bandits* didn't occur to him until three days before he completed the novel.) He figures that if he's curious about what will happen next, the reader will be too. What is surprising to him will then likely also be surprising to the reader.

Leonard's admission that his plots are improvised as he goes along may seem odd coming from a writer whose novels are often hailed as models of invention. But just as he fooled the Detroit police into thinking their dialogue was tape-recorded, Leonard fools many into assuming his clever plots are worked out in advance. One reviewer, for example, praised the denouement in *LaBrava* for "plausibly resolv[ing] an ironic plot that was fully thought through before either writer or reader began."[13] In truth, the ending was suggested to him at the last moment by his wife, and the plot, as usual, developed only as the novel was being written.

Because he is not tied down to any continuing character or specific type of novel, Leonard has no preconceived notions as to the direction his story must take. This allows him the freedom to take advantage of the unforeseen, to proceed in an unplanned direction. His improvisational plots are also perfectly suited to his protagonists, who often stumble into unexpected situations and get sucked into the action. In addition, Leonard's openness allows for the emergence of so many "sleeper" characters, people like Walter Kouza, Jiggs Scully, Jackie Garbo, etc., who weren't planned as major characters but who sprang to life on the page and demanded a larger role.

"If I were a half-decent narrative writer," Leonard admits, "I wouldn't adopt the storytelling method that I do."[14] His method of compensating for his narrative deficiency is to devote all his attention to his characters, who then take over the task of storytelling for him. As soon as he hears their voices clearly, interesting things begin to happen to propel the story along. Aside from an occasional slackness at the beginning (e.g., *Cat Chaser*) or in the middle of a novel (e.g., *Bandits*), his technique usually produces a well-paced novel with plenty of surprises and satisfying twists.

Despite the unplanned method of their composition, Leonard's novels are far from shapeless. Though he begins without a definite plot in mind, Leonard takes great care in the organization of individual scenes, rearranging them to achieve the best pace and rhythm and the most effective balance between action and exposition. If there is too much exposition in one scene, he will break it up by intercutting it with another scene. *Freaky Deaky* originally opened with the reunion scene between Robin and Skip in which they talk about the good old days. Sensing that this was too much exposition at the beginning of the novel, Leonard shifted scenes in order to begin with Chris Mankowski's last day on the job. Now action precedes exposition.

Leonard also takes care in shaping individual scenes. Many of his scenes end with a punch line, a zinger that puts a finishing touch on the preceding action or dialogue. He also takes care to get the right perspective for each scene, often rewriting from a different perspective to achieve better effect. As an experienced writer of screenplays, Leonard knows the importance of moving a story scene by scene. Few do it better than he does.

3. BE NATURAL: A corollary to his philosophy of "letting it happen" is "let it happen naturally." Leonard avoids situations that are artificial, contrived or clichéd. His readers will not get what convention dictates but what develops naturally out of the characters and the situation. He was inspired to write *Hombre,* for example, because of his impatience with all those "white flag" situations he was used to seeing on TV, where gunfighters followed the rules of polite gentlemen. In his novel, after John Russell's opponent approaches waving the white flag of surrender, Russell shoots him in the back as he walks away. One gets the sense that this is exactly how such a scene would be played out in real life.

Leonard's novels have such a natural quality about them because he rigorously avoids stereotypes and clichés. In his books personal confrontations between characters don't always result in fisticuffs or gunplay, as they invariably do in the works of lesser writers who lazily depend on formula. Leonard likes to avoid the expected. He also likes the unexpected when it comes to violence in his books. In *Bandits,* for example, Franklin de Dios walks up behind Jerry Boylan and shoots him in the head while he's standing at a urinal. His action is shocking simply because it is so surprising. And so realistic.

Leonard also avoids anything gimmicky in his prose. A writer like himself who takes such care to eliminate his own voice from his novels isn't going to do anything showy to draw attention to his writing. In *The Switch* a character comments on a local TV sportscaster's hokey attempt to sound like W. C. Fields reporting a Detroit Tiger victory: "Why don't they just say it, without all that cute shit?"[15] he asks. Leonard's writing never contains any "cute shit." No clever images, no fancy descriptions, no flowery langauge. Some of his characters (e.g., Barry Stam in *Stick* or Jackie Garbo in *Glitz*) might try hard to be cute, but that's because of who *they* are. Leonard himself is never cute, never showboaty.

Mauice Zola's assessment of Joe LaBrava's photography expresses this quality of Leonard's prose: "He's not pretentious like a lot of 'em. . . . You don't see any bullshit here. He shoots barefaced fact. He's got the feel and he makes *you* feel it."[16] Later in that novel, Joe LaBrava quotes from a newspaper review of his photographs: "The aesthetic sub-text of his work is the systematic exposure of artistic pretension."[17] This is exactly what the *Village Voice* reviewer said about Leonard's work.[18] LaBrava's put-down, "I thought I was just taking pictures" is not so much a repudiation of the critic's statement about Leonard's avoidance of pretense than a comment on the pretentious way he said it.

Leonard's artistic success isn't a matter simply of doing a little research and following a few rules of composition. If it were that easy, anybody could write as well as he does. It takes genius to do it as well as Leonard. It also takes a particular kind of genius to create humor as effectively as he does. Juvenal, the stigmatic hero of *Touch,* says that "being serious doesn't mean you have to be solemn."[19] Leonard's novels are about serious matters—murder, kidnapping, extortion, robbery—but their presentation is often exhilaratingly funny.

Leonard's characters are the primary source of humor. Their actions aren't ordinarily comic, but their words (and often their unspoken comments about what others say) frequently are. Leonard's novels abound with snappy one-liners ("I spent most of my dough on booze, broads and boats and the rest I wasted";[20] "Jerry wasn't the brightest guy I ever married";[21] "If bullshit was worth anything, Jack, you'd have the fertilizer market sewed up")[22] and brilliant exchanges between characters:

"How come you broke the guy's arm?"
"I didn't mean to. He raised it to protect his head."[23]

Or,

"You never said a kind word about mama in your life."
"I couldn't think of any."[24]

Or,

"I read in the paper that in the U.S., I think it was just this country, a woman is beaten or physically abused something like every eighteen seconds."
Roy said, "You wouldn't think that many women get out of line, would you?"[25]

Some of the biggest laughs come from the monologues of his great talkers, characters like Walter Kouza, Jiggs Scully, or Jackie Garbo. Leonard uses monologues far more sparingly than George V. Higgins. He resists the temptation to let his talkers go on too long and upset the balance of the novel. But when he has a character with the gift of gab, he knows how to use him to great effect.

The key to Leonard's humor is that the comic lines are usually spoken by characters who aren't intentionally funny. With a few notable exceptions like Barry Stam in *Stick,* Leonard's characters don't try to be funny. They just are, in a deadpan manner. One reason Leonard disliked the film version of *Stick* was that the actors paused after their lines for a laugh, or smirked as they delivered the lines. For best effect, his lines must be read straight, for they are spoken by characters who aren't aware that what they say is humorous. However, because of their attitudes and distinct speech mannerisms, what they say often makes one laugh.

Leonard currently enjoys a reputation as America's greatest living crime writer. And deservedly so. While it may be going a bit too far to claim, as one reviewer did, that "Leonard very well may be, strictly in terms of literature, one of the most meaningful and important writers working today,"[26] he has no peer when it comes to writing uncompromisingly realistic novels about crime and criminals.

Leonard is characteristically modest in describing his artistic aims: "My purpose is to entertain and tell a story,"[27] he declares simply. But as a proven master of storytelling, he has a genuine talent for keeping the reader hungrily turning the pages while offering him great entertainment along the way. But like many others who write realistic crime fiction, Leonard is more than a mere entertainer; he's also a social historian.

His crime novels paint a colorful portrait of an often overlooked segment of American life (perhaps more correctly, American lowlife). His subject isn't life among the rich and famous, or as it is lived behind the well-tended front lawns of suburbia. He's staked out as his territory the shadowy borderline between the cops and the crooks. His characters are usually simple people—jewel thieves and chauffeurs, blackmailers and process servers, con artists and morticians' assistants—who must work for a living. It's just that in his books, many of these individuals pursue occupations that take them outside the law. Out of such characters Leonard has created a series of novels noted for their drama, excitement, humor, thrills, and plain human interest.

Some have attempted to explain Leonard's popularity in terms of the rising crime rate in America. Roger Kaplan in *Commentary* argued that "Leonard's popularity . . . has increased as the Hobbesian view of society that his novels project has gained adherents."[28] John Sutherland, in the *London Review of Books,* voiced a similar notion: "In its popularity, Leonard's fiction answers to a widely-held sense of hopelessness about the bad guys. You can't beat them."[29]

But the fact is that his novels would likely be just as popular (and certainly just as good) if there were no crime in them at all. The success of his work isn't due to any increase in crime in America but rather to his ability to make his criminals come alive. Though his characters are frequently involved in crime, his primary focus is always on the person instead of the crime. A specific crime only serves to bring out the features of an individual—greed, revenge, a hankering for excitement—that make that person so fascinating to read about.

Choosing Leonard's best novel is difficult (Peter S. Prescott argues that "the margin of difference between Leonard's better and lesser works would admit, with difficulty, a butterfly's wing").[30] The overall excellence and consistent quality of his fiction is impressive. The novels since *City Primeval* are particularly rich in texture, colorful setting, and vivid characterization, and they contain some of the most entertaining dialogue in the business. The best of these—*Split Images, Cat Chaser, Stick, LaBrava, Glitz, Freaky Deaky*—are among the finest crime novels ever written.

Leonard's fiction represents a major achievement in crime writing. Though his novels do not belong to the Dashiell Hammett–Raymond Chandler school of hard-boiled writing, they do belong on the same shelf with the works of those two other giants. For the sake of convenience, novels by all three writers are usually shelved in the mystery sections of bookstores and public libraries. The fact is, however, in their artistry, originality, and impact, Leonard's novels deserve a permanent place beside those of Hammett and Chandler on the shelf marked simply Outstanding American Fiction.

Notes

1. "Who Is Elmore Leonard?"

1. Ken Tucker, "The Author Vanishes," *Village Voice,* 23 February 1982, 41.
2. J. D. Reed, "A Dickens from Detroit," *Time* 123 (28 May 1984), 84.
3. Peter S. Prescott, "Making a Killing," *Newsweek* 105 (22 April 1985), 62.
4. Elmore Leonard interview with author.
5. "Elmore Leonard's Shady Characters," *New York Daily News,* 25 May 1986.
6. Gregg Sutter, "Dutch," *Monthly Detroit* 3 (August 1980), 56.
7. Bob McKelvey, "Write on Target," *Detroit Free Press Magazine,* 19 August 1984, 16.
8. Prescott, "Making a Killing," 63.
9. Bruce Cook, "Elmore Leonard's Detroit Sound," *Washington Post Book World,* 7 February 1982, 5.
10. Chuck Potter, "Elmore Leonard," *Wichita Eagle-Beacon,* 22 June 1986.
11. Ibid.
12. David Hay, "After Dashiell Hammett Comes the Dickens from Detroit," *Good Weekend: The Sydney Morning Herald Magazine,* 20 July 1985, 51.
13. Leonard interview with author.
14. Sutter, 56.
15. Ben Yagoda, "Elmore Leonard's Rogues' Gallery," *New York Times Magazine,* 30 December 1984, 22.
16. Ibid.
17. Sutter, 58.

18. "Great Escapes: Writers Pick Their Favorites," *Washington Post Book World,* 7 December 1986, 5.
19. Janette Beckman, "Manic in Detroit," *New Musical Express,* 26 July 1986, 54.
20. Robert F. Jones, "Elmore Leonard," *People* 23 (4 March 1985), 76.
21. Ibid.
22. John Grossmann, "High Drama of Low Life," *American Way,* 5 February 1985, 44.
23. J. Anthony Lukas, "Elmore Leonard under the Boardwalk," *GQ* 54 (December 1984), 295.
24. Ibid., 260.
25. Dan Cryer, "Elmore Leonard, on a Roll," *Newsday Magazine,* 21 April 1985, 21.
26. Newgate Callendar, "Criminals at Large," *New York Times Book Review,* 4 April 1976, 34.
27. Callendar, "Decent Men in Trouble," *New York Times Book Review,* 22 May 1977, 33.
28. Jane Clapperton, "Cosmo Reads the New Books," *Cosmopolitan* 183 (August 1977), 19.
29. Jon Stewart, "*Glitz* Blitz," *Monthly Detroit* 8 (July 1985), 74.
30. Yagoda, 26.
31. *The New Yorker,* 12 July 1982, 107.
32. Michele Slung, "The Well-tuned, Precision Fuel-injected Thriller," *Washington Post Book World,* 4 July 1982, 4.
33. Allan Jones, "Elmore Leonard: *Cat Chaser,*" *Melody Maker,* 4 October 1982.
34. Jonathan Yardley, "Elmore Leonard: Making Crime Pay in Miami," *Washington Post Book World,* 20 February 1983, 3.
35. George Stade, "Villains Have the Fun," *New York Times Book Review,* 6 March 1983, 41.
36. Neal Johnston, "A Maze in Miami," *New York Times Book Review,* 27 November 1983, 26.
37. Yagoda, 22.
38. "Elmore Leonard: An Interview," *The New Black Mask Quarterly,* no. 2 (New York: Harcourt Brace Jovanovich), 11.
39. Yagoda, 29.
40. Leonard, Book-of-the-Month-Club Speech, Detroit, 27 June 1985.

41. Kathleen Silvassy, "A Decent Man and Not a Bad Writer," UPI Arts & Entertainment, 23 January 1987.
42. Grossmann, 44.
43. Michael Kernan, "Quiet Man of Mystery," *Washington Post Book World,* 6 February 1985, C1.
44. Bob Greene, "Solving the Mystery of Doing Whodunits," *Chicago Tribune,* 6 August 1985, sec. 5, 1.
45. Leonard interview with author.
46. Leonard, Book-of-the-Month-Club speech.
47. "Elmore Leonard: An Interview," 12.

2. Apache Apprenticeship

1. Elmore Leonard, "Trail of the Apache," *Argosy,* December 1951, 110.
2. Ibid., 111.
3. Leonard interview with author.
4. Elmore Leonard, *The Bounty Hunters* (New York: Bantam, 1979), 70.
5. Ibid., 71.
6. Elmore Leonard, *Hombre* (New York: Ballantine, 1961), 157.
7. Ibid., 40.
8. Ibid., 190.
9. Ibid.
10. Leonard, "Trail of the Apache," 23.
11. Elmore Leonard, "The Boy Who Smiled," in *The Arbor House Treasury of Great Western Stories,* ed. Bill Pronzini and Martin H. Greenberg (New York: Arbor House, 1982), 343.

3. From Cowboys to Cops and Robbers

1. "Elmore Leonard on *The Big Bounce,*" *Mysterious News,* September 1986, 1.
2. Leonard interview with author.
3. Yagoda, 22.
4. Bill Kelley, "This Pen for Hire," *American Film* 10 (December 1984), 56.

4. Crime Begins to Pay

1. Elmore Leonard, *Fifty-Two Pickup* (New York: Delacorte, 1974), 55.
2. Ibid., 73.
3. Elmore Leonard, *Glitz* (New York: Arbor House, 1985), 161.
4. Leonard, *Fifty-Two Pickup,* 121.
5. Prescott, "Making a Killing," 64.
6. Elmore Leonard, *Swag* (New York: Delacorte, 1976), 16.
7. Ibid., 39.
8. Ibid., 200.
9. Ibid., 55.
10. *Publishers Weekly* 209 (26 January 1976), 281.
11. Callendar, "Criminals at Large," 4 April 1976, 34.
12. Leonard interview with author.
13. Elmore Leonard, *Unknown Man No. 89* (New York: Delacorte, 1977), 4.
14. Elmore Leonard, *The Switch* (New York: Bantam, 1978), 155.
15. Kathy Warbelow, "You'll Like *Switch*—It's So Local," *Detroit Free Press,* 2 July 1978, 12C.
16. Elmore Leonard, *Touch* (New York: Arbor House, 1987), 135.
17. Ibid., 139.
18. Leonard interview with author.

5. Moving South: From Michigan to Miami

1. Elmore Leonard, *Gold Coast* (New York: Bantam, 1980), 4.
2. Ibid., 215.
3. Ibid., 178.
4. Ibid., 218.
5. Paul Wilner, "The Literary World Finally Considers Elmore Leonard a 'Serious Novelist,' " *Los Angeles Herald Examiner,* 3 February 1985.
6. Alvin P. Sanoff, "A Taste for Life's Seamy Side," *U.S. News & World Report* 102 (9 March 1987), 64.
7. Elmore Leonard, *City Primeval* (New York: Avon, 1982), 126.
8. Ibid., 199.
9. Ibid., 174.
10. Ibid., 24.

11. Ibid., 40.
12. Ibid., 148.
13. Ibid., 14.
14. Ibid., 88.
15. Ibid., 89.
16. Elmore Leonard, *Gunsights* (New York: Bantam, 1979), n.p. foll. 184.
17. Leonard, *City Primeval,* 156.
18. Ibid., 90.
19. Ibid., 27.
20. Elmore Leonard, *Split Images* (New York: Arbor House, 1981), 15.
21. Leonard interview with author.
22. Leonard, *Split Images,* 22.
23. Ibid., 251.
24. Ibid., 27.
25. Ibid., 259.
26. Ibid., 135.
27. Ibid.
28. Tucker, "The Author Vanishes," 41.
29. Larry Kart, "Magnifying Glass Finds a Deeper Mastery of Mystery in Leonard's *Split Images,*" *Chicago Tribune,* 10 February 1982, sec. 4, 7.
30. Elmore Leonard, *Cat Chaser* (New York: Arbor House, 1982), 204.
31. Ibid., 206.
32. Ibid., 114.
33. Ibid., 246.
34. Leonard interview with author.
35. Leonard, *Cat Chaser,* 166.
36. Cryer, "Leonard, on a Roll," 21.
37. Callendar, "Crime," *New York Times Book Review,* 5 September 1982, 20.
38. Robert Morales, "Leonard Da Vinci," *Heavy Metal,* January 1984, 4.
39. *New Yorker* 58 (12 July 1982), 107.

6. Fame and Fortune, Finally

1. Elmore Leonard, *Stick* (New York: Arbor House: 1983), 214.
2. Ibid., 174.
3. Ibid., 217.
4. Ibid., 109.
5. Ibid., 76.
6. Michael Kilgore, "Wounded Heroes and Tough Talk," *Tampa Tribune,* 1 June 1986, 8G.
7. Leonard, *Stick,* 128.
8. Ibid., 183.
9. Yardley, "Making Crime Pay in Miami," 3.
10. Kelley, "Pen for Hire," 53.
11. Yagoda, 20.
12. Elmore Leonard, *LaBrava* (New York: Arbor House, 1983), 46.
13. Ibid., 64.
14. Ibid., 14.
15. Ibid., 68.
16. Ibid., 168.
17. Lukas, "Under the Boardwalk," 259.
18. David Lehman, "Playing for Keeps," *Newsweek* 105 (4 February 1985), 80.
19. Christopher Lehmann-Haupt, "Books of the Times," *New York Times,* 4 February 1985, C20.
20. Chris Goodrich, "All That Glitters," *San Francisco Examiner,* 3 February 1985.
21. Stephen King, "What Went Down When Magyk Went Up," *New York Times Book Review,* 10 February 1985, 7.
22. James Crumley, "Leonard's *Glitz:* Sparkling, Solid." *USA Today,* 3 February 1985, 2D.
23. Prescott, "Making a Killing," 62.
24. Bob Greene, "A Writer's Writer Captures a Reader," *Chicago Tribune,* 5 August 1985, sec. 4, 1.
25. Elmore Leonard letter to Walter Mirisch, 17 October 1983.
26. Leonard interview with author.
27. Leonard, *Glitz,* 182.
28. Ibid., 141.
29. Ibid., 227.

30. R. Z. Sheppard, "Sleaze Factors," *Time* 125 (11 February 1985), 89.
31. Leonard, *Glitz,* 107.
32. Ibid., 194.
33. Ibid., 161.
34. Leonard interview with author.
35. Elmore Leonard, *Bandits* (New York: Arbor House, 1987), 201.
36. Ibid., 309.
37. Ibid., 342.
38. Ibid., 74.
39. Ibid., 239.
40. Ibid., 169.
41. Paul Gray, "Tough Talk and Local Color," *Time* 129 (12 January 1987), 72.
42. Frederic Koeppel, "Elmore Leonard Loses His Glitz with a Thriller That's All Shtick," *Memphis Commercial Appeal,* 11 January 1987.
43. Tom Dowling, "Bogged Down in a Swamp and Lost on a Reservation," *San Francisco Examiner,* 3 February 1987.
44. Leonard, *Bandits,* 326.
45. Beaufort Cranford, "Will Success Spoil Elmore Leonard," *Michigan: The Magazine of the Detroit News,* 9 October 1983, 11.
46. Leonard interview with author.
47. Elmore Leonard, *Freaky Deaky* (New York: Arbor House/William Morrow, 1988), 40.
48. Ibid., 42.
49. Ibid., 68.
50. Ibid., 70.
51. Ibid., 130.
52. Ibid., 136.
53. Ibid., 211.

7. "Why Is Elmore Leonard So Good?"

1. Walker Percy, "There's a Contra in My Gumbo," *New York Times Book Review,* 4 January 1987, 7.
2. Donald Westlake, "*LaBrava,*" *Washington Post Book World,* 13 November 1983, 1.

3. Lukas, "Under the Boardwalk," 295.
4. Reed, "Dickens from Detroit," 84.
5. Mike Lupica, "St. Elmo's Fire," *Esquire* 107 (April 1987), 170.
6. Christopher Lehmann-Haupt, "Books of the Times," *New York Times,* 4 February 1985, C20.
7. McKelvey, "Write on Target," 16.
8. Leonard, *Gold Coast,* 30.
9. Raymond Chandler, *The Simple Art of Murder* (New York: Ballantine, 1972), 16.
10. Leonard, Book-of-the-Month-Club speech.
11. Lukas, "Under the Boardwalk," 261.
12. Sanoff, "Life's Seamy Side," 64.
13. Johnston, "A Maze in Miami," 12.
14. Stewart, "*Glitz* Blitz," 106.
15. Leonard, *The Switch,* 99.
16. Leonard, *LaBrava,* 9.
17. Ibid., 101.
18. Tucker, "The Author Vanishes," 41.
19. Leonard, *Touch,* 173.
20. Leonard, *LaBrava,* 16.
21. Ibid., 150.
22. Leonard, *Bandits,* 341.
23. Leonard, *LaBrava,* 224.
24. Leonard, *Stick,* 181.
25. Leonard, *Bandits,* 113.
26. Fred Lutz, "Writer Dutch Leonard Merges Art with Hard-boiled Realism," *Toledo Blade,* 17 August 1986.
27. "Elmore Leonard: An Interview," 10.
28. Roger Kaplan, "Hard Guys and Heroes," *Commentary* 82 (May 1985), 64.
29. John Sutherland, "Number 1 Writer," *London Review of Books,* 5 September 1985, 16.
30. Prescott, "Making a Killing," 63.

Bibliography

1. Works by Leonard

A. Novels

The Bounty Hunters. Boston: Houghton Mifflin, 1953.
The Law at Randado. Boston: Houghton Mifflin, 1954.
Escape from Five Shadows. Boston: Houghton Mifflin, 1956.
Last Stand at Saber River. New York: Dell, 1959.
Hombre. New York: Ballantine, 1961.
The Big Bounce. New York: Fawcett, 1969.
The Moonshine War. New York: Doubleday, 1969.
Valdez Is Coming. New York: Fawcett, 1970.
Forty Lashes Less One. New York: Bantam, 1972.
Mr. Majestyk. New York: Dell, 1974.
Fifty-Two Pickup. New York: Delacorte, 1974.
Swag. New York: Delacorte, 1976. [rpt. as *Ryan's Rules*. New York: Dell, 1976.]
The Hunted. New York: Dell, 1977.
Unknown Man No. 89. New York: Delacorte, 1977.
The Switch. New York: Bantam, 1978.
Gunsights. New York: Bantam, 1979.
City Primeval. New York: Arbor House, 1980.
Gold Coast. New York: Bantam, 1980.
Split Images. New York: Arbor House, 1981.
Cat Chaser. New York: Arbor House, 1982.
Stick. New York: Arbor House, 1983.
LaBrava. New York: Arbor House, 1983.
Glitz. New York: Arbor House, 1985.

Dutch Treat. New York: Arbor House, 1985. [reprints *City Primeval, The Moonshine War, Gold Coast.*]
Double Dutch Treat. New York: Arbor House, 1986. [reprints *The Hunted, Swag, Mr. Majestyk.*]
Bandits. New York: Arbor House, 1987.
Touch. New York: Arbor House, 1987.
Freaky Deaky. New York: Arbor House/William Morrow, 1988.

B. Short Stories

"Trail of The Apache." *Argosy,* December 1951.
"Apache Medicine." *Dime Western,* May 1952.
"You Never See Apaches. . . ." *Dime Western,* September 1952.
"Red Hell Hits Canyon Diablo!" *10 Story Western Magazine,* October 1952. [pub. under name E. J. Leonard, Jr.]
"The Colonel's Lady." *Zane Grey's Western,* November 1952.
"Cavalry Boots." *Zane Grey's Western,* December 1952.
"Law of the Hunted Ones." *Western Story Magazine,* December 1952.
"Under the Friar's Ledge." *Dime Western,* January 1953.
"The Rustlers." *Zane Grey's Western,* February 1953.
"Three-Ten to Yuma." *Dime Western,* March 1953. Reprinted in *The Killers,* edited by Peter Dawson (New York: Bantam, 1955.)
"The Big Hunt." *Western Story Magazine,* April 1953.
"Long Night." *Zane Grey's Western,* May 1953.
"The Boy Who Smiled." *Gunsmoke,* June 1953. Reprinted in *The Arbor House Treasury of Great Western Stories,* edited by Bill Pronzini and Martin H. Greenberg (New York: Arbor House, 1982).
"The Hard Way," *Zane Grey's Western,* August 1953. Reprinted in *Branded West,* edited by Don Ward (Boston: Houghton Mifflin, 1956).
"The Last Shot." *Fifteen Western Tales,* September 1953.
"Trouble at Rindo's Station." *Argosy,* October 1953.
"Blood Money." *Western Story Magazine,* October 1953.
"Saint With a Six-Gun." *Argosy,* October 1954.
"The Captives." *Argosy,* February 1955.
"No Man's Guns." *Western Story Roundup,* August 1955.
"The Rancher's Lady." *Western Magazine,* September 1955. Reprinted

in *Wild Streets,* edited by Don Ward (Western Writers of America, 1958).
"Jugged." *Western Magazine,* December 1955.
"Moment of Vengeance." *Saturday Evening Post,* 21 April 1956.
"Man With the Iron Arm." *Complete Western Book,* September 1956.
"The Longest Day of His Life." *Western Novel and Short Stories,* October 1956.
"The Nagual." *2-Gun Western,* November 1956.
"The Kid." *Western Short Stories,* December 1956.
"Bull Ring at Blisston." *Short Stories Magazine,* August 1959.
"Only Good Ones." *Western Roundup,* edited by Nelson Nye (New York: Macmillan, 1961).
"The Tonto Woman." *Roundup,* edited by Stephen Overholser (Garden City: Doubleday, 1982).

C. Screenplays

The Moonshine War. MGM, 1970.
Joe Kidd. Universal, 1972.
Mr. Majestyk. United Artists, 1974.
High Noon Part II: The Return of Will Kane. Charles Fries, 1980. (CBS)
Stick. Universal, 1985.
52 Pick-Up. Cannon, 1986.
The Rosary Murders. Take One Productions, 1987.
Desperado. Universal, 1987. (NBC)

D. Nonfiction

"Commentary on *LaBrava*." *The New Black Mask Quarterly, No. 2*. New York: Harcourt Brace Jovanovich, 1985, 27–29.
"Elmore Leonard on *The Big Bounce*." *Mysterious News,* September 1986, 1–4.
"Impressions of Murder." *Detroit News Magazine,* 12 November 1978, 12.
"Introduction" to *Detroit* by Balthazar Korab (Charlottesville: Thomasson-Grant, 1986).

E. Interviews

"Elmore Leonard: An Interview." *The New Black Mask Quarterly, No. 2.* New York: Harcourt Brace Jovanovich, 1985, 1–12.

Kelley, Bill. "This Pen for Hire." *American Film,* December 1984, 52–56.

Lyczak, Joel M. "An Interview with Elmore Leonard." *The Armchair Detective,* Summer 1983, 235–240.

Martin, Roger. "Entretien avec Elmore Leonard." *Hard-Boiled Dicks, No. 17* (October 1986), 9–18. [In French]

Sanoff, Alvin P. "A Taste for Life's Seamy Side." *U.S. News & World Report,* 9 March 1987, 64.

Skinner, Robert E. "To Write Realistically: An Interview with Elmore Leonard." *Xavier Review,* 7:2 (1987), 37–46.

"Whodunit? Three Writers Spill the Beans." *Detroit News,* 30 November 1980, 1D. [also features Loren D. Estleman and William Coughlin]

Wholey, Dennis, ed. *The Courage to Change: Personal Conversations About Alcohol with Dennis Wholey.* New York: Warner Books, 1986, 87–94.

F. Manuscript Collection: University of Detroit Library

II. Selected Works about Leonard

Beckman, Janette. "Manic in Detroit." *New Musical Express,* 26 July 1986, 14.

Cook, Bruce. "Elmore Leonard's Detroit Sound." *Washington Post Book World,* 7 February 1982, 5.

Cranford, Beaufort. "Will Success Spoil Elmore Leonard?" *Michigan: The Magazine of the Detroit News,* 9 October 1983, 10–18.

Cryer, Dan. "Elmore Leonard, On a Roll." *Newsday Magazine,* 21 April 1985, 19–23.

Current Biography Yearbook, 1985. New York: H. W. Wilson, 1985, 264–68.

Dunn, Bill. "Elmore Leonard." *Publishers Weekly,* 25 February 1983, 32–33.

Fay, Stephen. "Sent Up for Stretches of Perfect Crime." *Sunday Times Magazine* (London), 16 June 1985, 48.

Greene, Bob. "Solving the Mystery of Doing Whodunits." *Chicago Tribune,* 6 August 1985, Sec. 5, 1.

———. "A Writer's Writer Captures a Reader." *Chicago Tribune,* 5 August 1985, Sec. 4, 1.

Grella, George. "Elmore Leonard." In *Twentieth-Century Crime and Mystery Writers,* Second Edition, edited by John M. Reilly. New York: St. Martin's, 1985, 558–59.

Grossmann, John. "High Drama of Low Life." *American Way,* 5 February 1985, 43–47.

Hamill, Pete. "King of the Genre." *New York Daily News Magazine,* 21 April 1985, 11.

Hay, David. "After Dashiell Hammett Comes the Dickens from Detroit." *Good Weekend: The Sydney Morning Herald Magazine,* 20 July 1985, 49–51.

Jolidon, L. A. "Murder, He Wrote." *USA Weekend,* 31 October–2 November 1986, 4–5.

Jones, Robert F. "Elmore Leonard." *People,* 4 March 1985, 73–80.

Kernan, Michael. "Quiet Man of Mystery." *Washington Post Book World,* 6 February 1985, C1.

Kilgore, Michael. "Wounded Heroes and Tough Talk." *Tampa Tribune,* 1 June 1986, 1G.

Lukas, J. Anthony. "Elmore Leonard Under the Boardwalk." *GQ,* December 1984, 259.

Lupica, Mike. "St. Elmore's Fire." *Esquire,* April 1987, 169–172.

McKelvey, Bob. "Write on Target." *Detroit Free Press Magazine,* 19 August 1984, 14–17.

Mesplède, Claude. "De la piste solitaire à la jungle des villes." *Hard-Boiled Dicks, No. 17,* October 1986, 19–34. [In French]

Mitgang, Herbert. "Novelist Discovered After 23 Books." *New York Times,* 29 October 1983, 17.

Morley, Jefferson. "Middle-Class Hustlers." *The New Republic,* 25 March 1985, 38–40.

Most, Glenn. "Elmore Leonard: Splitting Images." *Western Humanities Review,* Spring 1987, 78–86.

Prescott, Peter S. "Making a Killing." *Newsweek,* 22 April 1985, 62–67.

Reed, J. D. "A Dickens from Detroit." *Time,* 28 May 1984, 84–86.

Shah, Diane K. "For Elmore Leonard, Crime Pays." *Rolling Stone,* 28 February 1985, 33.

Skinner, Robert E. *The New Hard-Boiled Dicks: A Personal Checklist.* Madison, IN: Brownstone Books, 1987, 37–42.

Stanford, Phil. "Elmore Leonard's South Beach Realism." *Marquee,* May 1984, 32–3.

Stewart, Jon. "*Glitz* Blitz." *Monthly Detroit,* July 1985, 72–75.

Sutter, Gregg. "Advance Man: Researching Elmore Leonard's Novels, Part 2," *The Armchair Detective,* Spring 1986, 160–172.

———. "Dutch." *Monthly Detroit,* August 1980, 54–58.

———. "Getting It Right: Researching Elmore Leonard's Novels, Part 1," *The Armchair Detective,* Winter 1986, 4–19.

Tucker, Ken. "The Author Vanishes." *Village Voice,* 23 February 1982, 41.

Yagoda, Ben. "Elmore Leonard's Rogues' Gallery." *New York Times Magazine,* 30 December 1984, 20–29.

Index